Jesus in India

Jesus' Deliverance from the Cross
&
Journey to India

Hadhrat Mirza Ghulam Ahmad of Qadian
THE PROMISED MESSIAH AND MAHDI,
FOUNDER OF THE AHMADIYYA MUSLIM JAMA'AT

ISLAM INTERNATIONAL PUBLICATIONS LTD.

Jesus in India

English Translation of *Masih Hindustan Mein*

First Edition (Urdu): 1908, Qadian
First English Version: 1944, Qadian
Reprints: 1962, Rabwah
              1973, Qadian
              1978, London
              1989, London
              1991, Qadian
              1995, London
Present Edition (Fully Revised):2003, London

Translated into English from Urdu by the late Qazi Abdul
Hamid and thoroughly revised by Professor Chaudhry
Muhammad Ali.

© Islam International Publications Ltd.

Published by:
    Islam International Publications Ltd.
    'Islamabad' Sheephatch Lane,
    Tilford, Surrey GU102AQ
    United Kingdom.

Composed by:
Raja Ata-ul-Mannan

Cover Designed by:
Mirza Nadeem Ahmad

Printed in U.K. at:
    Raqeem Press
    Tilford, Surrey

ISBN: 1 85372 723 7

Publisher's Note

Jesus in India is the English version of *Masih Hindustan Mein,* an Urdu treatise written by the Holy Founder of the worldwide Ahmadiyya Muslim Jamaat, Hadhrat Mirza Ghulam Ahmad (1835-1908), the Promised Messiah and Mahdi. The main thesis expounded in this treatise is Jesus' deliverance from death on the Cross and his subsequent journey to India in quest of the lost tribes of Israel whom he had to gather into his fold as foretold by Jesus himself.

Starting his journey from Jerusalem and passing through Nasibus and Iran, Jesus is shown to have reached Afghanistan where he met the Jews who had settled there after their escape from the bonds of Nebuchadnezzar. From Afghanistan Jesus went to Kashmir where some Israelite tribes had also settled. He made this place his home and here he died and lies buried in Srinagar, Kashmir.

In this book, Hadhrat Ahmad has solved another difficult problem which has for long confounded many a western writer, namely the problem of the resemblance between Christian and Buddhistic teachings and also between the life of Jesus and that of Buddha, as recorded in their respective Scriptures. Some of these writers hold that Buddhistic teachings must somehow have reached Palestine and were incorporated by Jesus in his own sermons. But there is absolutely no historical evidence to support this theory. A Russian traveller named Nicolas Notovitch stayed for quite some time with Lamas in Tibet and had their religious chronicles translated for him. He is of the opinion that Jesus must have been to Tibet before the Crucifixion and gone back to Palestine after having imbibed Buddhistic teachings.

Rejecting both these views, Hadhrat Ahmad proves that Jesus came to India only after the Crucifixion and not before, and that it was not he who borrowed Buddha's teachings but the Buddhists who seem to have reproduced the Gospels in their books. Jesus also visited Tibet during his travels in India in search of the lost tribes of Israel. He preached his message to Buddhist monks, some of whom were originally Jews. They were deeply impressed by Jesus' teachings and accepted him as the manifestation of the Buddha, the Promised Teacher. With faith in him as their Master, they incorporated his teachings into the teachings of the Buddha himself.

Masih Hindustan Mein, was—it still is—an epoch-making and cataclysmic book. It transformed the theological landscape of Judaism, Pauline Christianity and conventional Islam. The catalyst it introduced was that Jesus—a true prophet of God that he was, was saved from death on the cross, lived long and lies buried in Srinagar Kashmir.

As stated in the Introduction and at the end, the book was to be divided into two parts, the first to comprise as many as ten chapters plus an epilogue, and the second part to contain additional proofs of Jesus' journey to India and a comparative evaluation of the teachings of Islam and Christianity establishing the truth of Islam as well as of his own claim to be the Promised Messiah. It seems he couldn't find time for further research on this subject, but he made good his resolve by ushering in a spiritual rebirth of Islam in its pristine purity, founding the dynamic Ahmadiyya Muslim Jamaat worldwide and writing not one but more than eighty books concerning the truth of Islam, his own claim as the Promised Messiah and Mahdi and the life and death of Jesus.

Written in 1899, and partly serialized in *Review of Religions* in 1902 and 1903, the book itself was posthumously published on 20th November 1908. The first English translation, by the late Qazi Abdul Hamid, was published in 1944. On instructions from Hadhrat Mirza Tahir Ahmad, Khalifat-ul-Masih IV, Imam of the worldwide Ahmadiyya Muslim Jamaat, the present edition has been thoroughly revised by Professor Muhammad Ali Chaudhry, Wakilut Tasnif, Rabwah.

As supporting evidence of the theses advanced in this book, relevant excerpts from different authors and researchers are given at the end as appendix. These excerpts do not form part of the original text which, in the course of translation, has been kept inviolate and even misprints, if any, have not been corrected. The correct version has, however, been given in footnotes only after permission by our august Imam, Hadhrat Khalifa-tul-Masih IV. The author's footnotes are indicated by asterisks, while the translator's footnotes have been numbered 1,2,3, etc.

Since different editions of the Bible differ in the serial numbers of verses, care has been taken to stick to the numbers quoted by the author. Biblical references have been quoted from the Authorized King James' Version, published by the Zondervan Corporation, Grand Rapids, Michigan 49530, USA.

THE PUBLISHERS

Acknowledgments

We owe a debt of deep gratitude to all those who helped in the preparation of this revised edition of *Jesus in India*, particularly to Maulana Bashir Ahmad Akhtar, Mr. Dhulqarnain and Raja Ata-ul-Mannan for proof reading and verifying references and helping in a variety of ways.

We are also deeply grateful to Maulana Munir-ud-Din Shams, Additional Wakilut Tasnif, London and Mr. Arshad Ahmadi for scrutinizing and correcting the proofs, particularly Maulana Shams for his continued interest and useful suggestions. We are also grateful to Mr. Munwwar Saeed for preparing the index, and to the Arabic Desk in London, headed by Maulana Abdul Momin Tahir, for updating the Appendix.

Chaudhry Muhammad Ali
Wakilut Tasnif
Rabwah

vii

Table of Contents

بِسْمِ اللهِ الرَّحْمٰنِ الرَّحِيْمِ ¹

نَحْمَدُهُ وَ نُصَلِّى عَلٰى رَسُوْلِهِ الْكَرِيْمِ ²

رَبَّنَا افْتَحْ بَيْنَنَا وَ بَيْنَ قَوْمِنَا بِالْحَقِّ وَ اَنْتَ خَيْرُ الْفَاتِحِيْنَ

Our Lord! Decide between us and our people in truth;
For You are the One Who decides best.

Introduction

I have written this book so that by adducing proofs from established facts, conclusive historical evidence of proven value, and ancient documents of other nations, I might dispel the serious misconceptions which are current among Christians and most Muslim sects regarding the earlier and the later life of Jesus. The dangerous consequences of these misconceptions have not only hijacked and destroyed the concept of *Tauhid* – Divine Unity, but their insidious and poisonous influence has long been noticed in the moral condition of Muslims in this country. It is these baseless myths and tales that result in spiritual maladies, like immorality, malice, callousness, and cruelty, which are almost endemic among most Islamic sects. Virtues like human sympathy, compassion, affability, love of justice, meekness, modesty, and humility are disappearing by the day, as if they will soon bid a hasty farewell to them. This

---

¹ In the name of Allah, the Gracious, the Merciful. [Translator]
² We praise Allah and invoke His blessings upon His noble Prophet[sa]. [Translator]

callousness and moral degradation makes many a Muslim appear only marginally different from wild beasts. A Jain[3] or a Buddhist is afraid of killing even a mosquito or a flea and detests such an act, but alas! there are many among Muslims who would kill an innocent person with impunity and commit wanton murder without the least fear of God Almighty Who rates human life higher than all other animals. Why then this callousness, cruelty, and lack of sympathy? It is because from their very childhood, myths and false stories regarding a false concept of Jihad are drummed into their ears and instilled into their hearts. As a result, they gradually become morally dead and cease to realize the heinousness of such abominable deeds. On the other hand, a man who murders an unsuspecting person and brings ruin to his family, thinks that he has done a meritorious and rightful deed and made the most of an opportunity to win social acclaim. This is because no sermons or lectures are delivered in our country to discourage such evils, and if at all there are any such sermons, they have an aura of hypocrisy about them; and the man in the street continues to think approvingly of such misdeeds. Hence, taking pity upon the plight of my people, I have already written books in Urdu, Persian and Arabic, in which I have proved that the popular concept of Jihad prevalent among Muslims, such as the expectation of a bloodthirsty Imam and cultivation of malice for others, are no more than false notions harboured by shortsighted clerics. Islam, on the contrary, does not allow the use of the

---

[3] Jainism is a religion of Indian origin which forbids harming any living creatures, whether humans, animals or insects. (Translator)

sword in religion except in the case of defensive wars, wars
which are waged to punish a tyrant, or those which are
meant to uphold freedom. The need of a defensive war
arises only when the aggression of an adversary threatens
one's life. Except for these three kinds of Jihad permitted by
the *Shariah* — Islamic law, no other kind of war is allowed by
Islam in support of religion. To highlight this concept of
Jihad, I have distributed books in this country and in
Arabia, Syria and Khurasan, etc., at great cost. But now, by
the grace of God, I have adduced arguments powerful
enough to dispel these unfounded beliefs from the people's
minds. I have found clear proofs and strong and conclusive
circumstantial and historical evidence, the light of whose
truth gives the tiding that, soon after their publication, there
will come about a welcome change in the hearts of the
Muslims. I am sure that after these truths have been
comprehended, sweet and refreshing springs of modesty,
humility and compassion will gush forth from the hearts of
the righteous sons of Islam. There will be a spiritual
transformation which will have a wholesome and benign
impact on the nation at large. I am also sure that Christian
scholars and all those who hunger and thirst after the truth,
will benefit from this book. And, as I have just pointed out,
the real object of this book is to correct the wrong beliefs
which have found their way into the creeds of the Muslims
and the Christians. However, this requires some elaboration
which is as follows.

Christians and most Muslims believe that Jesus was
raised to the heavens alive; both have believed for a long
time that Jesus is still alive in the heavens and will return to
the earth sometime in the latter days. The difference in the

views of Muslims and Christians is that Christians believe that Jesus died on the cross, was resurrected, went to heaven in his earthly body, seated himself on the right hand of his Father and will return to the earth for judgment in the latter days. They further say that Jesus, the Messiah, is the Creator and Master of the world and none other; he it is who, in the latter days, will descend to the earth in glory and majesty to pronounce reward and punishment. All those who do not believe in him or his mother as God, will be caught and thrown into hell, where crying and lamenting will be their lot. But the aforesaid sects of Muslims say that Jesus was never crucified, nor did he die on the cross. Instead, when the Jews arrested him for crucifixion, an angel of God took him to the heavens in his earthly body, and that he is still alive there, which according to them is the second heaven, where the prophet Yahya or John is also quartered. Muslims, moreover, believe that Jesus is an exalted prophet of God but not God, nor the Son of God. They also say that he will, in the latter days, descend to the earth, near the Minaret at Damascus, or elsewhere, supported by two angels. Jesus and Imam Muhammad — the Mahdi, who will be a Fatamite and will already be there in this world — will kill all non-Muslims, and will not spare anyone except those who become Muslims at once. In short, the real object of the second coming of Jesus to the earth, as stated by the Muslims known as Ahl-e-Sunnah and Ahl-e-Hadith, also called Wahabis by the common people, is that quite like the Mahadev[4] of the Hindus, he will destroy the whole world; and that he will first threaten people to

---

[4] One of the three great Hindu gods. (Translator)

become Muslims and, if they persist in their disbelief, shall put them all to the sword. They also affirm that he has been kept alive in the heavens in his earthly body, so that when Muslim powers become weak, he will come down and kill the non-Muslims or coerce them on pain of death to become Muslims. The divines of the aforesaid Muslim sect say, particularly about the Christians, that when Jesus comes down from the heavens, he will break all the crosses in the world, indulge in all sorts of cruel deeds with the sword, and fill the earth with blood. And, as stated before, the Ahl-e-Hadith and others from among the Muslims gleefully proclaim that shortly before the second coming of the Messiah, there will appear an Imam from among the descendants of Fatima[rz], whose name will be Muhammad, the Mahdi. He it is who will be the Khalifa and King of the time by virtue of his being one of the Quraish. Since his real object will be to kill all non-Muslims except those who readily recite the Kalima, Jesus will come down to give him a helping hand in this task; and although Jesus in his own right will be a Mahdi, indeed he will be the greater Mahdi, but since it is essential that the Khalifa of the time should be from among the Quraish, Jesus will not be the Khalifa. Instead, Muhammad, the Mahdi, will be the Khalifa. They further allege that the two of them together will fill the earth with human blood, and so much blood will be shed that it will be unprecedented in the history of the world. The moment they appear, they will start this bloody carnage, but they will neither preach nor plead, nor show any sign. They also say that although Jesus will be like an advisor or a helper to Imam Muhammad, the Mahdi, and although the reins of power will be in the hands of the Mahdi alone, Jesus will continue to instigate and incite Hadhrat Imam Muhammad, the Mahdi, to violence, as if he were trying to make up for the humane teaching he preached to the world before, i.e., not to resist evil, and on being struck on one cheek, to turn the other cheek also.

This, in sum, is the Muslim and Christian belief regarding Jesus. Although Christians are guilty of a grave error in calling a humble man God, some Muslims too, particularly the Ahl-e-Hadith, generally known as the Wahabis, believe in a bloodthirsty Mahdi and an equally bloodthirsty Messiah. This has corrupted their moral condition to the extent that neither can they live with other people in a climate of peace, trust, and good will, nor can they be truly and completely loyal to a non-Muslim government. Every reasonable man would understand that such a belief, namely, that non-Muslims should be subjected to coercion, and that they should either directly become Muslims or be put to death, is open to very serious objections. Human conscience spontaneously realizes that it is highly objectionable to convert a person to one's faith by coercion, and by threatening to kill him, without ever giving him the opportunity to understand the truth of a faith and apprising him of its moral teaching and values. Far from contributing to the growth of a religion, this would give the opponents the opportunity to find fault with it. The ultimate result of this kind of thinking is that hearts become devoid of human sympathy. Justice and compassion, which are some of the cardinal human values, become extinct, and spite and ill will begin to flourish; only brutality remains, wiping out all high moral qualities. But it is only too obvious that such teachings cannot be from God, Who punishes only after His message has been fully communicated.

Just imagine, would it be reasonable to simply kill a man if he does not accept the true faith, even though he is as yet ignorant and unaware of its truth and its noble and excellent message? Instead of answering his denial with the sword or the gun, such a man deserves compassion, and needs to be instructed gently and politely in the truth, beauty and the spiritual excellence of the faith. Hence, the view of Jihad held by these sects of Islam, and their belief that the time is near when there will arise a bloodthirsty Mahdi named Imam Muhammad, that the Messiah will come down from the skies to lend him a helping hand, and that the two of them together will kill all non-Muslims if they deny Islam, is utterly opposed to moral sense. Doesn't this belief put all good human qualities and morals out of action, and excite beastly passions. Those who hold such beliefs have to lead a life of hypocrisy with others, so much so that they cannot even give true loyalty to their rulers. The allegiance they profess is a lie. That is why some of the Ahl-e-Hadith sects mentioned above are living a double life under the British Government in India. In secret, they hold out hopes to the common people of the coming of the bloody days of a bloodthirsty Mahdi and Messiah, and preach accordingly, but to the rulers they go as sycophants, assuring them that they do not approve of such ideas. But if they are really sincere, why do they not express their disapproval in their writings, and why do they await the coming of the bloodthirsty Mahdi and Messiah so impatiently as if they were standing at the doorstep, eager to join him?

It is because of such beliefs that the moral fiber of these clerics has suffered so much deterioration. They are no longer capable of preaching peace and compassion. On the other hand, they consider it their prime religious duty to go about killing others. I would be glad if any sect of the Ahl-e-Hadith is opposed to these beliefs, but I cannot help observing with regret that among the sects of the Ahl-e-Hadith* there are Wahabis incognito who believe in a bloodthirsty Mahdi and in the common concept of Jihad. They believe what is contrary to the true faith, and, if the opportunity offers, they consider it virtuous to kill people who profess other religions. Whereas the truth is that belief in killing others in the name of Islam, or in prophecies like the one about the bloody Messiah or wishing to advance the cause of Islam by bloodshed and threats, is absolutely against the Holy Quran and authentic *Ahadith*. Our Holy Prophet[sa] suffered great hardship in Mecca and thereafter at the hands of the disbelievers. The thirteen years which he spent at Mecca were years of great affliction and suffering. Even to think of them brings tears to one's eyes. But he did not raise the sword against his enemies, nor did he reply in kind to their abuse, until many of his disciples and close friends were mercilessly killed, and he was himself subjected to all kinds of persecution. He was poisoned many a time; and many an unsuccessful attempt was made

---

* Some of the Ahl-e-Hadith write in their books unjustly and with great impertinence that the birth of the Mahdi is imminent: that he will put the British rulers of India behind the bars, and that the Christian king will be brought before him as prisoner. Such books are still extant in Ahl-e-Hadith homes. *lqtiraab-us-Sa'ah* is one of these books, whose author is a well-known Ahl-e-Hadith scholar. Vide page 64 of this book. (Author)

to murder him. When, however, God's vengeance came, it so happened that the Meccan and tribal chiefs decided unanimously that this man, the Holy Prophet^{sa}, should at all events be put to death. It was at that time that God, who is the Supporter of His loved ones and of the truthful and the righteous, informed him that nothing but evil was left in the town, that the people were bent upon murdering him and that he should leave the town at once. Then in response to divine command, he migrated to Medina. Even there, his enemies did not leave him alone; they pursued him, and tried at all costs to annihilate Islam. When their arrogance exceeded all limits, and their crime of killing innocent people had made them only too fit to be punished, Muslims were given the permission to fight in self-defense. And those people and their helpers did deserve punishment for killing many innocent persons and robbing them of their possessions, not in any fair fight or battle, but out of sheer mischief. But in spite of all this, when Mecca was taken, our Holy Prophet^{sa} pardoned them all. It is, therefore, utterly wrong and unfair to suppose that the Holy Prophet^{sa} or his companions ever fought to spread Islam, or forced anyone to join its fold.

Remember, at the time all nations were highly prejudiced against Islam. The enemy was scheming to destroy Islam which he thought was a new religion and the followers of which were only a negligible minority, and everyone was anxious to see the Muslims destroyed at the earliest, or too torn apart to have any possibility of growth. This is why the Muslims had to encounter hostility at every step, and anyone from any tribe who accepted Islam was either summarily killed by his tribe or lived in perpetual danger of

losing his life. At this juncture, God Almighty took pity on
Muslim converts, and imposed on the bigoted powers the
penalty of becoming subjects of the Islamic state, thereby
throwing open the doors of freedom for Islam. This was
meant to remove the obstructions in the way of those who
wished to accept the faith; it was God's mercy upon
mankind, and did no one any harm.

It is evident, however, that non-Muslim rulers today do
not interfere with the religious freedom of Muslims; they do
not restrict the carrying out of religious rites; do not kill new
converts to Islam from among their own people and do not
put them into prison or torture them. Why then should
Islam permit the use of the sword against them? For a fact,
Islam has never advocated compulsion in religion. If you
closely study the Holy Quran, books of *Hadith* and historical
records, and examine them and reflect upon them as far as
possible, you will realize that the charge that Islam ever
used force and wielded the sword to spread the faith is an
utterly unfounded and shameless allegation. Such charges
are levelled against Islam by people who have not been able
to read the Quran, *Hadith* and the authentic chronicles in an
objective and impartial spirit, and have made free use of
slander and falsehood. I know the time is approaching fast
when those who are hungry and thirsty for truth will come
to know of the reality of these slanderous charges. How can
we describe Islam as a religion of compulsion, when its
Holy Book, the Holy Quran, unequivocally commands:

⁵ لَآ اِكْرَاهَ فِى الدِّيْنِ

---

⁵ 2 : 257 (Translator)

This means that you are simply not allowed to convert people by force. Can we ever accuse the great Prophet Muhammad[sa] of using force, while, for thirteen long years of his Meccan life, he continued to exhort his companions not to return evil for evil, but to forbear and forgive? When mischief exceeded all limits, and everyone joined hands to try to obliterate Islam, God's wrath required that those who kill by the sword should be killed by the sword. Except for this, the Holy Quran does not at all approve of compulsion. Were it so, the companions of our Holy Prophet[sa], in moments of trial, would not have succeeded in proving their sincerity as true believers. While the loyalty of the companions of our Master, the Holy Prophet[sa], is a matter upon which I hardly need to dwell, it is no secret that the examples of upholding the truth and loyalty displayed by the disciples are unparalleled in the history of other nations. This band of the faithful did not waver in their loyalty and steadfastness even under the shadow of the sword. The unrelenting steadfastness they exhibited in the company of the Holy Prophet[sa] is not humanly possible unless one's heart is lit up with the light of genuine belief. In short, there is no room for compulsion in Islam. Wars in Islam fall under three categories:

i. Defensive war — war by way of self-protection;
ii. Punitive war — blood for blood;
iii. War to establish freedom — to break the hold of those who kill converts to Islam.

Whereas Islam does not permit that anyone should be converted by force or by threat to one's life, it is simply absurd to await the appearance of a bloodthirsty Mahdi and

Messiah. It is impossible that, contrary to the teaching of the
Holy Quran, someone should appear and convert people to
Islam by force. Now, this was not something that defied
comprehension or was too difficult to understand. Only the
ignorant have been led to this belief because of selfishness.
Most of our clerics happen to labour under the delusion that
wars waged by the Mahdi will bring great wealth, so much
so, that they will not be able to handle it. Since most of the
Maulvis or Muslim clerics today are so hard up, they are
eagerly waiting for the Mahdi to appear, who, they think,
will satisfy their baser appetites. Little wonder, therefore, if
these people turn against anyone who does not believe in
the appearance of such a Mahdi. Such a person is at once
denounced as an apostate, and outside the pale of Islam. For
these very reasons I too am an apostate in their eyes, since I
do not believe in the coming of a bloodthirsty Mahdi and
Messiah and I detest such absurd beliefs. But this is not the
only reason why they denounce me as an apostate. Of
course, I do not believe in the coming of an imaginary
Messiah and Mahdi. But there is also an added reason,
which is that I have publicly proclaimed that God has
revealed to me that the real Promised Messiah who is also
the Mahdi, tidings of whose appearance are to be found in
the Bible and the Holy Quran and whose coming is also
promised in the *Ahadith* is none other than myself.
However, I have come without a sword or a gun; God has
commanded me that with meek and gentle humility and
peace I should invite people to God Who is True, Eternal
and Immutable and is the Most Holy, All-Knowing, Ever-
Merciful, and Just.

I alone am the light of this age of darkness. He who

follows me will be saved from falling into the pits prepared by the Devil for those who walk in the dark. I have been sent by God to lead the world in humility and peace to the True God, and to re-establish the reign of moral values in Islam. God has provided me with heavenly signs for the satisfaction of seekers after truth, and has shown miracles in my support. He has disclosed to me secrets of the unseen and of the future which, according to the Scriptures are the real criteria for judging and identifying the true claimant to this divine office. He has vouchsafed to me true Knowledge and comprehension of verities. That is why, souls which hate truth and love darkness have turned against me. But it was my desire to be kind and forgiving towards mankind, as far as it lay in my power. Hence, in this age the greatest sympathy one can show to the Christians is to draw their attention to the True God Who transcends the traumas of birth, death, pain and suffering. He created all primordial matter and particles in spherical shapes, and thus signed this inherent message in nature that, like every sphere, His own being is One. He is not subject to any dimensions. None of the expansive bodies have been created triangular. All the things God created in the beginning, the earth, the heavens, the sun and the moon, the stars, the elements, are all spherical in shape; this denotes Unity and Oneness of the Creator. Hence there can be no truer sympathy and love for the Christians than that their attention should be invited towards the God Whose handiwork absolves Him of the taint of trinity.

The one good service one could do to the Muslims would be to reform their moral condition. Efforts should be made to dispel the false hopes which they entertain in connection

with the appearance of a bloodthirsty Mahdi and Messiah.
Such expectations are entirely against the teachings of
Islam. I have just said that the ideas of some of the present
day Muslim clerics that there will appear a bloody Mahdi,
who will spread Islam at the point of the sword, are
contrary to the Quranic teachings and are only the result of
wishful thinking. For a right-minded and truth-loving
Muslim to shed such beliefs, it should be enough that he
study the Holy Quran closely, pause, consider and see that
the Holy Word of God is very much against threatening to
kill people if they fail to become Muslims. This one
argument alone is sufficient to refute such false notions.
Nevertheless, out of a feeling of sympathy, I have decided
to refute the aforesaid misconceptions by clear and positive
proofs from history and other sources. Hence, I shall try to
prove in this book that Jesus did not die on the cross, nor
did he go up to the heavens; nor should it be supposed that
he would ever again come down to the earth. On the
contrary, the fact of the matter is that he died at the age of
120 years at Srinagar, Kashmir, where his tomb is still to be
found in the Khan Yar quarter. To prove this point, I have
divided this enquiry into ten chapters and an epilogue,
which are as follows:

1. Testimonies from the Gospels.
2. Testimonies from the Holy Quran and the *Ahadith*.
3. Testimonies from medical literature.
4. Testimonies from historical records.
5. Testimonies from oral traditions which have been
   handed down from generation to generation.
6. Testimonies from miscellaneous circumstantial
   evidence.

7. Testimonies from logical argument.
8. Testimonies from the fresh revelation I have received from God.

These constitute eight chapters. In chapter 9, there will be a brief comparison between Christianity and Islam, setting out arguments in favour of the latter. In chapter 10, there will be a somewhat detailed account of the aims and objectives which I have been divinely commissioned to realize. This will include evidence to prove that I am the Promised Messiah and that I have been sent by God. At the end, there is an epilogue in which I have set forth some important guidelines.

I trust that those who read this book will do so carefully, and will not reject, out of prejudice, the truth contained in it. I should like to remind that this is not a cursory and passing investigation; the proofs contained in this book have been made available after a deep and searching inquiry. I pray to God that He may help me in this undertaking and lead me by His special revelation and inspiration to the perfect Light of truth, for all true knowledge and clear perception descend from Him, and only with His leave can it guide human hearts to truth. Amen!

MIRZA GHULAM AHMAD,
Qadian
25th April 1899

بِسْمِ اللّٰهِ الرَّحْمٰنِ الرَّحِيْمِ

Chapter One

Christians believe that Jesus was arrested and crucified, owing to his betrayal by Judas Iscariot, was later resurrected, and raised to heaven. A detailed study of the Gospel, however, disproves this notion altogether. It is written in Matthew chapter 12 verse 40:

For as Jonah was three days and three nights in the whale's belly; so shall the son of man be three days and three nights in the heart of the earth.

Now it is obvious that Jonah did not die in the belly of the whale; all that happened was that he went into a swoon or a coma. The holy books of God bear witness that Jonah, by the grace of God, remained in the belly of the whale alive, came out alive, and his people ultimately accepted him. If then Jesus had died in the belly of the whale,[6] what resemblance could there be between the dead and the living, and vice versa? The truth is, that Jesus was a true prophet and he knew that God, who loved him, would save him from an accursed death. Therefore, on the basis of divine revelation, he prophesied in the form of a parable, and positively intimated that he would not die on the cross, nor would he give up his ghost on the accursed wood; on the contrary, like the prophet Jonah, he would only be in a state of swoon. In the parable, he had also hinted that he

---

[6] This is a misprint in the first edition, the word 'whale' should be read 'earth'. [Translator]

would come out of the bowels of the earth and join his
people and would be honoured like Jonah. This prophecy
was also fulfilled; for Jesus came out of the bowels of the
earth and went to his tribes who lived in the eastern
countries like Kashmir and Tibet. These were the ten tribes
of the Israelites who 721 years* before Jesus, had been taken
captive and forced to leave Samaria by Shalmaneser, King
of Assur. They eventually came to India and settled in
various parts of the country. Jesus had to make this journey,
for the divine object underlying his mission was to meet the
lost tribes of Israel who had settled in different parts of
India. This was because these were the lost sheep of Israel
who had renounced their ancestral faith after settling in
these parts, and most of them had become Buddhists, and
gradually started worshipping idols. Dr. Bernier, on the
authority of a number of eminent scholars, states in his
Travels that the Kashmiris in reality are the Jews who had
migrated to this country during the political turmoil in the
days of the king of Assur.**7 In any case, it was incumbent
upon Jesus to find out the whereabouts of the lost sheep,
who had got mixed with the local people after coming to
India. I shall presently produce evidence to prove that Jesus
did in fact come to India and then, by stages, travelled to
Kashmir, and discovered the lost sheep of Israel among
Buddhists, who ultimately accepted him the way Jonah was
accepted by his people. This was inevitable, for Jesus
himself said in so many words that he had been sent to the

---

* Besides these, more Jews were exiled to eastern countries as a result of
Babylonian excesses. (Author)
** See Volume II of *Travels* by the Frenchman Dr. Bernier. (Author)
7 See Appendix extract 10. (Translator)

lost sheep of Israel.

Otherwise too, he must needs have escaped death on the cross, for it was stated in the Holy Book that whoever was hanged on the cross was accursed. The term 'accursed' has a connotation which it would be cruel and unfair to apply to a chosen one of God like Jesus, for, according to the agreed view of all whose mother tongue is Arabic, *la'nat*, or curse, has reference to the state of one's heart. A man is said to be accursed when his heart, having been estranged from God, becomes dark; when, deprived of divine mercy and of divine love, devoid absolutely of His knowledge, blind and deaf like Satan, he is saturated with the poison of unbelief; when there remains not a ray of divine love and knowledge in him; when the bonds of love and loyalty are broken, and, between him and God, mutual hatred and disdain and spite and hostility take root, so much so that they become enemies; and God becomes weary of him and he becomes weary of God; in short, he becomes an heir to all the attributes of the Devil. That is why the Devil himself is called the accursed.[*]

The connotation of the word 'accursed' is so foul and unclean that it can never apply to a righteous person who entertains the love of God in his heart. It is a pity that Christians did not consider the significance of curse when they invented this belief; otherwise, they could never have used such a degrading word for a righteous man like Jesus. Can we ever possibly imagine that Jesus' heart was estranged from God; that he had denied His existence,

---

[*] Vide the lexicons: Lisaan-ul-Arab, Sihah Jauhari, Qaamus, Muhit, Taj-ul-Urus, etc. (Author)

hated Him and had become His enemy? Can we ever imagine that Jesus ever felt in his heart of hearts that he was alienated from God, that he was an enemy of God, and that he was totally lost in the darkness of unbelief and denial? But while Jesus never experienced such feelings and his heart was always full of the light of Divine love and knowledge, then, my worthy intellectuals, how can we ever say that not one, but thousands of curses descended upon Jesus with all their evil significance! God forbid, this could never be. How then can we believe that Jesus was accursed? What a pity, that once a man has expressed an opinion or taken his stand on a certain doctrine, he is ill-inclined to turn back from it, even if all its ills are exposed before him. It is praiseworthy indeed to seek salvation if it is based on authentic reality, but where is the sense in a desire for salvation which kills truth and countenances the belief regarding a holy prophet and perfect man, that he passed through a state in which he was totally estranged from God, and instead of unreserved and single-minded submission, there appeared in him a strangeness and alienation, even enmity and hatred, and that darkness filled his heart in place of light?

Remember, this kind of thinking not only detracts from the dignity of the prophethood of Jesus but is also derogatory to his claim to spiritual eminence, holiness, love, and knowledge of God, to which he gives repeated expression in the Gospels. Just look it up in the New Testament where Jesus claims that he is the Light and the Guide of the world, that he has a relationship of great love with God, that he has been blessed with a pure birth and that he is the beloved son of God. How then, in spite of these pure and holy ties, can the unholy attributes of a curse be ascribed to Jesus? No, this can never be so. There cannot be the least doubt therefore that Jesus was not crucified, and did not die on the cross, for his person did not deserve the stigma of death on the cross. Not having been crucified, he was also spared the unclean consequence of the curse, and this no doubt proves that he did not physically go to heaven. Since ascension was a constituent part of the whole scheme and a corollary of crucifixion, it necessarily follows that as he was neither accursed nor did he go to hell for three days, nor for that matter did he die on the cross, the second part of the scheme, namely, that of ascension, also stands nullified. The Gospels contain even more evidence on this, which I proceed to set below. One of these is the following statement of Jesus:

> But after I am risen again, I will go before you into Galilee.
> (Matthew 26: 32)

This verse clearly shows that Jesus, after he had come out of the sepulchre, went to Galilee and not to heaven. His words 'After I am risen' do not mean coming to life after being dead; rather, Jesus used these words in anticipation of what the people were going to say in the future, because as it turned out, they thought he had died on the cross. And indeed, if a man is put on the cross, with nails driven into his hands and feet, and he faints away for all his suffering, looking more dead than alive; if such a man is saved from his ordeal and recovers his senses, it would hardly be an exaggeration on his part to say that he had come to life again. No doubt, Jesus' escape from such a predicament was no less than a miracle. There is no doubt that after so much suffering, Jesus' escape from death was a miracle, but it would be wrong to say that Jesus had actually died. True, words to this effect are of course found in the Gospels, but this is only the kind of mistake which the evangelists have also made in the recording of several other historical events. In the light of their research, commentators of the Gospels admit that the books of the New Testament can be divided into two parts:

i. The religious teaching which the disciples received from Jesus; this constitutes the essence of the teachings of the Gospel.

ii. Historical events, like the genealogy of Jesus, his arrest and his being beaten; the existence at the time of a miraculous pond, etc., were recorded by the writers on their own authority. They were not revelations but were written down according to the writers' own perceptions. At places, we find gross exaggerations, for instance, it is stated that if all the miracles and works of Jesus were put into writing, the world would not be big enough to accommodate them. What a hyperbole!

On the other hand, it would be quite in keeping with common parlance to describe as death the traumatic shock suffered by Jesus. This kind of expression is almost universal. Whenever a man escapes from such a near-fatal experience, without any hesitation he is considered to have been given 'a new life'.

One thing more worth attention is that in the Gospel of Barnabas, which should be available in the London library, it is written that he was not put on the cross, nor did he die thereupon. We could very well point out that though this book is not included in the Gospels and has been rejected summarily, but there is no doubt that it is an ancient book, and was written at the same time as the other Gospels. Can't we, therefore, view this book as an ancient chronicle and make use of it as an historical document? And can't we conclude from this book that at the time when the event of the cross took place, people were not unanimous as to Jesus having died on the cross? Apart from this, the four Gospels themselves use metaphors describing a dead person as being asleep. It is not far from the point to suppose that coma has been described as death. As I have already mentioned, a prophet never lies. Jesus compared his three days' stay in the tomb to the three days Jonah spent in the belly of the whale. This only shows that just as Jonah remained alive in the belly of the whale for three days, Jesus must also have been alive in the tomb for three days. It must be remembered here that the Jewish tombs in those days were not like the present-day tombs; they were spacious like a room and had an opening at one end covered with a big stone. I shall prove in due course that Jesus' tomb, which has been recently discovered in Srinagar in Kashmir, is exactly similar to the one in which Jesus was placed in a state of swoon.

In short, the verse I have just quoted shows that Jesus, after coming out of the sepulchre, went to Galilee. It is written in the Gospel of Mark that after coming out of the sepulchre, Jesus was seen on the road to Galilee, and in due course he met the eleven disciples who were at their meal; he showed them his hands and feet which bore wounds; they thought that he was perhaps a spirit. Then he said to them: 'It is I myself; touch me and see for a spirit has no flesh and bones as I have.' Then he took a piece of broiled fish, and of an honeycomb and ate it before them. See Mark 16:14 and Luke 24:39-42. [8]

These verses show that it is certain that Jesus never went to the heavens; rather, he came out of the sepulchre and went to Galilee like a common man, in ordinary clothes and a human body. If he had been resurrected after death, how was it that his spiritual body could still have borne the wounds inflicted upon him on the cross? What need had he to eat? And if he required food then he must be in need of food even now!

Readers should know better than to think that the Jewish cross was like the present day gallows, from which deliverance is almost an impossibility. In those days, no noose was secured around the neck of the victim, nor was the wooden plank pulled from under him to keep him hanging. Instead, the victim was put on the cross, his hands and feet were nailed to it; and there was always the possibility that after he was put on the cross and duly nailed, he could still be taken down alive after a day or two, before his bones had been broken, in case it was decided to

---

[8] "Afterward he appeared unto the eleven as they sat at meat, and upbraided them with their unbelief and hardness of heart, because they believed not them which had seen him after he was risen." – Mark 16:14 "And as they thus spake, Jesus himself stood in the midst of them, and saith unto them, Peace *be* unto you. But they were terrified and affrightened, and supposed that they had seen a spirit. And he said unto them, Why are ye troubled? and why do thoughts arise in your hearts? Behold my hands and my feet, that it is I myself: handle me, and see; for a spirit hath not flesh and bones, as ye see me have. And when he had thus spoken, he showed them *his* hands and *his* feet. And while they yet believed not for joy, and wondered, he said unto them, Have ye here any meat? And they gave him a piece of a broiled fish, and of an honeycomb. And he took *it*, and did eat before them." – Luke 24:36-43 (Translator)

spare his life, the punishment already undergone being considered sufficient. If he was meant to be killed, he was kept on the cross, was denied food and water and left in this condition under the sun for at least three days, after which his bones were broken and he would expire under the torture. But by the grace of God Almighty, Jesus was spared the agony which would otherwise have meant certain death. A close scrutiny of the Gospels would reveal that neither did Jesus remain on the cross for three days, nor did he have to suffer hunger or thirst, nor were his bones broken. On the contrary, he remained on the cross only for about two hours, and it so happened, by the grace of the Almighty, that he was placed on the cross in the latter part of the day, which was a Friday, sometime before sunset, the next day being the Sabbath, the Jewish feast of Fasah. Now, according to Jewish custom, it was unlawful and a cognizable offence to let anyone remain on the cross on the Sabbath, or the night before. Jews, like Muslims, followed the lunar calendar, according to which the day began with the sunset. On the one hand was this welcome circumstance which was born of earthly causes, and, on the other, divine scheme intervened. When the sixth hour had struck, a severe dust storm began to blow which enveloped the world in darkness and persisted for at least three hours. See Mark 15:33. The sixth hour was after twelve o'clock and was close to evening. Now, the Jews got worried at the deep darkness and feared lest the night of the Sabbath should overtake them and lest, having violated the sanctity of the Sabbath, they should be deservedly punished. Therefore, they hurriedly removed Jesus and the two thieves from their crosses. In addition to this, there was another heavenly intervention. When Pilate presided at his court, his wife sent word to him saying, Have nothing to do with that just man (don't seek to have him killed) for I have suffered many things in a dream because of him. See Matthew 27:19.[9] So, this angel, whom the wife of Pilate saw in her dream, would have us and all fair-minded people believe, that God had never intended for Jesus to die on the cross. Ever since creation, it has never happened that God should reveal to a person in a dream that a particular thing would happen in a certain way, and still that thing should fail to happen. For example, Matthew says that an angel of the Lord came to Joseph in a dream and said:

> Arise, and take the young child and his mother, and flee into Egypt, and be thou there until I bring thee word: for Herod will seek the young child to destroy him. (Matthew 2:13)

Can anyone imagine that Jesus could have been killed in Egypt? The dream of Pilate's wife was similarly a part of divine design, which could never fail in its objective. Just as the possibility of Jesus being put to death during the journey to Egypt was against the specific promise of God, so here too it is unthinkable that the angel of God should appear to Pilate's wife and point out to her that if Jesus died on the cross it would spell disaster for her, and yet the angel's appearance should go in vain, and Jesus should be allowed to suffer death on the cross. Is there any example of this in the world? None. The pure conscience of all good men, when informed of the dream of Pilate's wife, will no

---

[9] "When he was set down on the Judgement seat, his wife sent unto him, saying, Have thou nothing to do with that just man: for I have suffered many things this day in a dream because of him." – Matthew 27:19 (Translator)

doubt testify that for a fact it was the purpose of the dream to lay the foundation for Jesus' rescue. On the other hand, everyone is free to reject a self-evident reality, out of sheer prejudice for his creed, but fairness would have us believe that the dream of Pilate's wife is a piece of weighty evidence in support of Jesus' escape from the cross. Matthew, the first and foremost of the Gospels, testifies to this. Although the powerful evidence which I shall set out in this book at once invalidates the divinity of Jesus and the doctrine of Atonement, yet honesty and fairness demand that we should pay no heed to our people, family, and conventional religion in accepting the truth. Since his creation, man, because he lacked true insight, has deified very many objects, so much so, that even cats and snakes have been worshipped. But the wiser among men, by the grace of God, have always managed to keep away from such polytheistic beliefs.

Among the testimonies of the Gospels, which testify to Jesus' escape from death on the cross, is the journey he undertook to a far-off place i.e. Galilee after coming out of the sepulchre. On Sunday morning, the first person he met was Mary Magdalene, who at once informed the disciples that Jesus was alive, but they did not believe her. Then he was seen by two of the disciples who were walking in the countryside; and finally he appeared to all the eleven while they were at their meal and remonstrated with them for their callousness and lack of faith. See Mark 16:9-14. Again, when the disciples were going towards the hamlet called Emmaus, 3.75 *kose*[10] from Jerusalem, Jesus joined them; and

---

[10] Different scales are used to measure distance in different parts of the

when they reached the hamlet, Jesus wanted to part company with them, but they insisted on his staying. He then dined with them, and they all spent the night with Jesus in Emmaus. See Luke 24:13-31. Now, it is absolutely impossible and irrational to say that Jesus ate and drank and slept and made a journey of about 70 *kose* to Galilee and performed all the functions of the physical body with a disembodied spirit—the spiritual form the human body assumes after death. Although many differences are found in the Gospels due to differing dispositions, they clearly prove that Jesus met his disciples in his mortal, physical body, and made a long journey on foot to Galilee. He showed his wounds to the disciples, had the evening meal with them, and slept in their company. We shall later on prove that he even treated his wounds with a special ointment.

Now, one has to consider, as to how it is possible that after a person has been invested a glorious and eternal frame, and exempted from the necessity of eating and drinking, is to sit on the right hand of God, and freed from all pain and deformity, he should still bear on his hands and feet fresh nail wounds which bleed and hurt, and an ointment has to be prepared to heal them? In other words, even after having an eternal body which should last forever without changing or deteriorating, Jesus was still suffering from a number of travails. He even showed his flesh and bones to his disciples; he was also prone to hunger and thirst, or it would serve no purpose to eat and drink and to

---

world. According to the measurement mentioned by the Promised Messiah in this book, one *kose* is equal to 1.625 miles. (Translator)

rest during his journey. Food and water are indeed necessary for mortal bodies in this world, and their lack could prove fatal. Hence, there is no doubt that Jesus did not die on the cross, and did not acquire a new spiritual body: rather, he was in a state of coma which resembled death. And it so happened, by God's mercy, that the tomb in which he was placed was not like the tombs we have in this country; it was a large and ventilated room with an opening. It was a custom with the Jews in those days to build large sepulchers with an access; they were kept ready and when someone died, his body was placed there. We find a clear testimony of this in the Gospels. Luke says,

> Now upon the first day of the week very early in the morning, they (the women) came unto the sepulchre bringing the spices which they had prepared, and certain others with them. And they found the stone rolled away from the sepulchre and they entered in and found not the body of the Lord Jesus. (Luke 24:2-3)[11]

Consider for a moment the words, 'they entered'. Obviously, a man can only enter a tomb which is like a room and has an opening. I shall again state at its proper place in this book that the tomb of Jesus which has recently been discovered in Srinagar, Kashmir, also has an opening This is a very special point and researchers can draw meaningful conclusions from it.

Among the testimonies of the Gospels are the words of Pilate, recorded by St. Mark:

> And now when the even was come, because it was the preparation, that is the day before the Sabbath, Joseph of

---

[11] This seems to be a misprint in the first edition. The correct reference is Luke 24:1-3. [Translator]

Arimathea, an honourable counsellor, who also waited for
the kingdom of God, came, and went in boldly unto Pilate,
and craved the body of Jesus. And Pilate marvelled if he were
already dead. (Mark 16: 42-44)[12]

This shows that suspicion had risen at the very moment
of crucifixion as to whether Jesus had actually died, and this
suspicion was raised by a person who knew well enough
how long it took for a person to die on the cross.

Among the testimonies of the Gospels are also the
following verses:

The Jews, therefore, because it was the preparation, that the
bodies should not remain upon the cross on the Sabbath day
(for that Sabbath day was an high day), besought Pilate that
their legs might be broken, and that they might be taken
away. Then came the soldiers and brake the legs of the first,
and of the other which was crucified with him. But when
they came to Jesus and saw that he was dead already they
brake not his legs: But one of the soldiers with a spear
pierced his side, and forthwith came there out blood and
water. (John 19:31-34)

These verses clearly show that in order to put an end to
the life of a crucified person, it was the practice in those
days to keep him on the cross for several days, and then to
break his legs, but Jesus' legs were purposely not broken,
and he was taken down alive from the cross, like the two
thieves. That was the reason why blood gushed out when
his side was pierced, whereas the blood of a dead man is
congealed. This shows very clearly that there was some
kind of a secret plan. Pilate was a God-fearing and good-

---

[12] This is a misprint in the first edition. The correct reference is Mark
15:42-44) [Translator]

hearted man; he could not openly show favour to Jesus for fear of Caesar because the Jews condemned Jesus as a rebel. All the same, Pilate was lucky to have beheld Jesus but Caesar was not so fortunate. Pilate not only saw Jesus but also showed him great favour. He did not at all desire that Jesus should suffer crucifixion. It is clear from the Gospels that Pilate resolved several times to let Jesus go, but the Jews threatened that if he did so, he would be disloyal to Caesar because, according to them, Jesus was a rebel who wanted to become king. (John 19:12)

Moreover, the dream which Pilate's wife saw, was also the prime mover to the effect that somehow or the other, Jesus should be saved from crucifixion, and that it would otherwise spell disaster. Since the Jews were a mischievous people, and were quite ready to report him to Caesar, Pilate used a subterfuge to release Jesus. First, he ordered Jesus' crucifixion in the expiring hours of a Friday, close to the night of Sabbath. Pilate was only too well aware that according to the Jewish law Jesus could only be kept on the cross until that evening, as the Sabbath would then begin and it would be unlawful to keep the bodies on the cross. It is unthinkable that the two thieves should be alive after two hours and Jesus should be dead; this was rather part of the design not to allow Jesus' bones to be broken. To a person with some common sense, it is indeed a reasonable point to ponder that the two thieves were taken down alive from their crosses. Indeed, it was normal practice that people were taken down alive from the cross and died only when their bones were broken or they breathed their last because of hunger and thirst after staying on the cross for a few days. But Jesus had to suffer none of these travails. Neither was he kept on the cross hungry and thirsty for so many days, nor were his bones broken to put a stop to his life at once. It would be understandable if even one of the two thieves had died and there had been no need to break his bones.

Furthermore, Joseph, a close friend of Pilate's, who was a chief in those parts, and a secret disciple of Jesus, happened to arrive at this very moment. I presume that he too was summoned by Pilate. Jesus was declared dead and his body was placed in his custody. Since Joseph was a respected personality, the Jews could not quarrel with him. Thus, he took charge of Jesus, who had been declared dead whereas he was actually in a coma. Following Pilate's instructions, he took Jesus to a room with an opening which was used as a grave according to the prevailing custom of the time, and was beyond the access of the Jews.

All this took place in the midst of the 14th century after the demise of the prophet Moses, and the Messiah was the divine reformer who was to revive the Jewish faith in that century. Although the Jews themselves were awaiting the Messiah in the fourteenth century, and the prophecies of the earlier prophets testified to his coming, it is a pity that the Jews did not recognize the person and the time and denounced their Promised Messiah as an imposter. They called him an apostate, pronounced a verdict of death against him, and dragged him to court. This shows that the fourteenth century has the inherent quality of making people's hearts callous, and causing religious clerics to become blind and averse to the truth. A comparison between the fourteenth century after Moses and the fourteenth century after the Holy Prophet[sa] — who is the similitude of Moses, will show, first, that in both of these centuries there was a man who claimed to be the Promised Messiah, and that it was a true claim, made on the authority of God Almighty. We also know that the religious leaders of the two peoples declared both of them to be apostates, denounced them as unbelievers and Anti-Christs, and pronounced verdicts of death against both. They were both taken to the courts; a Roman court in one case and a British court in the other. But in the end, they were both saved and the designs of both the Jewish and the Muslim clerics failed. God intended to raise great communities for both the Messiahs, and to defeat the designs of their enemies. In short, the fourteenth century after Moses and the fourteenth century after our Holy Prophet[sa], are both hard and trying and, in the long run, full of blessings for their respective Messiahs.

Among the testimonies which bear out that Jesus was indeed saved from the cross is the one narrated in Matthew 26:36-46. It relates that, having been informed by revelation of his impending arrest, Jesus prayed to God all night, crying and prostrating. These prayers, offered in such humility, for which Jesus was given ample time, could not have gone unaccepted. God never turns down the prayer of a chosen one when he prays in distress. How then could Jesus' prayer have been turned down, which he offered all night long in a state of anguish and distress, particularly when Jesus himself had announced that his Father in heaven listened to his prayers. How could we say that God listened to his prayers if this prayer offered in such distress was not accepted? The Gospels also show that Jesus was certain that his prayer had been accepted and that he had great faith in his prayer. That is why when he was arrested and put on the cross, and found the circumstances contrary to his expectations, he involuntarily cried out: ایلی ایلی لما سبقتانی 'Eli, Eli, lama sabachthani', that is to say 'My God, my God why hast Thou forsaken me?',[13] meaning, 'I did not expect things would come to this pass and that I would have to die on the cross. I was certain that God would listen to my prayers.' So, both these references of the Gospels show that Jesus firmly believed his prayer would be heard and accepted and his nightlong cries and supplications would not go in vain. In fact, he had himself taught his disciples, on divine authority, that if they prayed, their prayers would be accepted. He had also related the parable of the judge who feared neither God nor man, which was intended to convey to the disciples that God did indeed listen to prayers. Although Jesus had been apprised of the impending catastrophe, yet, like all righteous people, he prayed to God, believing that there was nothing impossible for Him and that everything that happened or did not happen was subject to God's will. Now if Jesus' own prayer was not accepted, God forbid, what an adverse effect this would have had on his disciples who had seen with their own eyes that the prayer of a great prophet like Jesus, addressed all night long with such burning passion, had not been accepted. Such an unfortunate example would have sorely tried their faith. God's mercy, therefore, desired that this prayer must be accepted; and the prayer offered at Gethsemane was indeed accepted.

---

[13] See Matthew 27:46 (Translator)

There is another point to remember in this connection. Just as there was a conspiracy to kill Jesus, for which purpose the chief priests and the scribes assembled at the palace of the high priest called Caiphas and devised a plan to kill Jesus, so was there a conspiracy to murder Moses, and, likewise, the Holy Prophet[sa], for which there was a secret consultation in Mecca at a place called Dar-ul-Nadwa. But God Almighty saved both the great prophets from the evil consequences of these designs. The conspiracy against Jesus lies, in point of time, between the two conspiracies; why then was Jesus not saved, even when he had prayed so earnestly and in a much more dire situation? Why was Jesus' prayer not heard, when God hears the prayers of His beloved servants and frustrates the designs of the wicked? All righteous people know by experience that the prayer of the distressed and the afflicted is accepted. Indeed the hour of distress is the time for the righteous to show signs. I have had personal experience of this. Two years ago, a false charge of attempted murder was brought against me by Dr. Martin Clark, a Christian, who was a resident of Amritsar, Punjab. The case was filed in the district court, Gurdaspur, and it was alleged that I had sent a person named Abdul Hameed to murder the said doctor. It so happened that I was opposed in this case by several scheming persons belonging to the three communities, Christian, Hindu, and Muslim, who joined hands in trying to prove the charge of attempted murder. The Christians were against me because I was trying, and am still trying, to rescue humanity from the false notions which Christians entertain regarding Jesus; and this was the first taste of their ire. The Hindus were displeased with me because I had made a prophecy regarding the death of Pundit Lekh Ram, with his consent, and the prophecy was fulfilled within the appointed time, which was indeed a terrible sign from God. Likewise, the Muslim clerics were angry because I was opposed to the idea of a bloodthirsty Messiah and to the doctrine of Jihad as understood by them. So, some important personages of these three communities counselled together to somehow prove the charge of murder against me, so that I should either be hanged or imprisoned. They were thus unjust in the sight of God. God had informed me of this long before their secret consultations, and had given me the tidings of my ultimate acquittal. These divine revelations were announced beforehand to hundreds of people; and when after the revelation, I prayed: 'Lord! Save me from this affliction,' it was revealed to me that God would save me and clear me of the charge brought against me. This revelation was verbally communicated to more than three hundred persons, many of whom are still alive. It so happened that my enemies produced false witnesses in the court, and very nearly 'proved' the case, witnesses of the three communities mentioned earlier having deposed against me. Then, it so happened, that the truth of the case was disclosed by God in a variety of ways to the magistrate before whom the case was pending. This magistrate was Captain W. Douglas, the Deputy Commissioner of Gurdaspur. He was convinced that the case was false. Then without caring for the doctor who was also a missionary, his sense of justice made him dismiss the case. Thus what I had announced about my acquittal on the authority of divine revelation to hundreds of people and in public meetings turned out to be true notwithstanding the mounting danger of the attending circumstances. This served to fortify the faith of many people. This was not all. More charges of this kind and calumnies of a criminal character were preferred against me on the above grounds, and cases were taken to court, but before I could be summoned, God informed me of the origin and the end of each affair, and in every case howsoever alarming, I was given the glad tidings of acquittal in advance.

The point of this discourse is that God Almighty does indeed accept prayers especially when the oppressed knock on his door with implicit faith in Him; He attends to their plaints, and helps them in strange ways. To this, I myself am a witness. Why was it then that the prayer of Jesus uttered in such anguish was not accepted? But indeed, it was accepted, and God did save him. God caused things to happen on earth and in heaven to rescue him. John, i.e. the Prophet Yahya, had no time to pray for his end had arrived, but Jesus had a whole night to pray, and he spent it in supplication, standing and prostrating before God, for God had willed that he should give expression to his distress and pray to Him for Whom nothing was impossible. So the Lord, in keeping with His eternal practice, heard his prayer. The Jews lied when they taunted Jesus at the time of the crucifixion as to why God had not saved him despite his trust in Him? God frustrated all the designs of the Jews and saved His beloved Messiah from the cross and the attending curse. And the Jews had indeed failed.

Among the testimonies of the Gospels which have reached us are the following verses from Matthew:

That upon you may come all the righteous blood shed upon the earth, from the blood of righteous Abel unto the blood of

Zacharias son of Barachias, whom ye slew between the temple and the altar. Verily I say unto you, All these things shall come upon this generation. (Matthew 23:35-36)

Now, if you think over these verses you will find that Jesus clearly says that the killing of prophets by the Jews ceased with the prophet Zacharias, and that after that, the Jews had no power to kill any prophet. This is a major prophecy which clearly points out that Jesus was not killed as a result of crucifixion; he was rather saved from the cross, dying ultimately a natural death. For if Jesus was also to suffer death at the hands of the Jews, like Zacharias, he would have hinted at it in these verses. If it is argued that Jesus was killed by the Jews but this was not a sin on the Jews' part, for Jesus' death was in the nature of an atonement, the contention is hardly tenable, for in John 19:11 Jesus says that the Jews have been guilty of a great sin for having resolved to kill him; and likewise in many other places there is the unmistakable hint that as a penalty for the crime of which they had been guilty against Jesus, they deserved punishment in the sight of God. See the Gospel[14] 26:24.

Among the testimonies of the Gospels which have reached us, is this verse in Matthew:

Verily I say unto you, There be some standing here, which shall not taste of death, till they see the Son of man coming in his kingdom. (Matthew 16:28)

And this verse from John:

Jesus saith unto him, If I will that he (the disciple John) tarry (in Jerusalem) till I come. (John 21:22)

---

[14] Gospel of Matthew. [Translator]

This means: 'If I will, John will not die till I come again'. These verses show with great clarity that Jesus had made a promise that some people would still be alive when he returned; among these, he had named John. The fulfillment of this promise was therefore inevitable. Accordingly, Christians also admit that for the prophecy to be fulfilled in accordance with the promise, it was inevitable that Jesus should have come at a time when some of his disciples were still alive. This is also the basis of the clergymen's declaration that Jesus had come to Jerusalem at the time of its destruction, as he had promised, and that John had seen him, as he was still alive at the time. But it should be noted that Christians do not say that Jesus really came down from heaven accompanied by appointed signs; they rather say that he appeared to John in a kind of vision so that he might fulfil his prophecy contained in Matthew 16:38.[15] But I say that such coming does not fulfil the prophecy. It is a very poor attempt at interpretation and is meant to avoid the objections inherent in the prophecy. This interpretation is evidently untenable and wrong, so much so, that it needs no refutation, for if Jesus had to appear to anyone in a dream or a vision, a prophecy of this kind would be ridiculous.[*]

---

15 This is a misprint in the first edition; the correct reference is 16:28. (Translator)

* I have seen in certain books interpretations of Matthew 26:24[16] by Muslim clerics which are more laboured than even the interpretations of Christians; they say that when Jesus declared it to be a sign of his coming that some people of that generation would still be alive and that a disciple would also be alive when the Messiah would appear, it is necessary that that disciple should be living up till now, for the Messiah has not come yet; and they think that that disciple is hiding somewhere on some mountain, awaiting the Messiah! (Author)

16 This is a misprint in the first edition; the correct reference is 16:28. (Translator)

Moreover, Jesus had also appeared to Paul long before this in the same manner. It appears that the prophecy contained in Matthew 16:28 has caused a panic among the padres and they have not been able to give it a rational meaning consistent with their own beliefs. It was difficult for them to say that Jesus, at the time of the destruction of Jerusalem, had descended from heaven in glory, and that, like the lightning which lights up the heavens, was seen by everybody; and also it was not easy for them to ignore the statement, 'Some of those who are standing here will not taste death till they have seen the Son of man coming in his kingdom.' Therefore, as a result of a laboured interpretation they believed in the fulfillment of the prophecy in the form of a vision. But this is not true; righteous servants of God always appear in visions to the divinely elect, and for a vision it is not even necessary that they should appear only in a dream, they can be seen even when one is awake, and I myself have experienced such phenomena. I have seen visions in which I met Jesus many a time, and I have also met some of the other prophets, while I was fully awake. I have also seen our Chief, Lord and Master, the Holy Prophet Muhammad[sa] many a time in this condition, and I have talked to him in such a clear state of being awake that sleep or drowsiness had nothing to do with it. I have also met some dead people at their graves or other places while I was awake, and have talked to them. I very well know that such a meeting with the dead in this state is possible, and that not only can we meet, we can also talk to them and even shake hands. Between this and the ordinary state of being awake there is no difference during such an experience; a person feels that he is in this very world, has the same ears, eyes and tongue, but deeper reflection reveals a different universe. The world cannot understand this kind of experience, for the world lies in a state of indifference. This experience is a gift of God for those who are endowed with an extra sensory perception. The experience is of course genuine and authentic. Therefore, when Jesus appeared to John after the destruction of Jerusalem, though the latter might have seen him while fully awake, and though they might have had some conversation and a handshake between them, nevertheless, the incident has nothing to do with the prophecy. Such phenomena often take place in the world and even now, if I devote some attention to it, I can by the grace of God see Jesus or some other holy prophet while I am awake. But such a meeting would not fulfil the prophecy contained in Matthew 16:28.

What actually happened was that Jesus knew that he would be saved from the cross and would migrate to another land, that God would neither let him die nor take him away from this world as long as he had not seen the destruction of the Jews with his own eyes, and that he would not die unless and until the kingdom of heaven, vouchsafed to the godly, realized its aims and objectives. Jesus made this prophecy to assure his disciples that they would presently see the sign that those who had raised the sword against him would be killed with the sword during his lifetime and in his very presence. Thus, if evidence is of any value, there is no greater evidence to convince the Christians than the fact that Jesus himself prophesied that some of them would still be alive when he returned.

Remember, the Gospels contain two kinds of prophecies about the coming of Jesus:

i. The promise of his coming in the latter days means his coming in the spiritual sense, like the coming of Elijah before the coming of the Messiah. Like Elijah, he has already appeared in this age and it is I, the writer, a servant of mankind, who has appeared in the name of the Messiah as the Promised Messiah. Jesus has told of my coming in the Gospels, and blessed is he who, out of love for Jesus, considers my claim with justice and fairness, and saves himself from going astray.

ii. The other prophecies regarding the second coming of Jesus mentioned in the Gospels constitute evidence of his life which continued after the experience of the cross, by the sheer grace of God. It was in accordance with the prophecy that God saved his chosen servant from death on the cross.

Christians are mistaken in mixing up these two contexts. Because of this, they end up confused and have to face many complications. The verse in chapter 16 of Matthew is, therefore, a very important piece of evidence in support of Jesus' escape from the cross.

Among the testimonies of the Gospels which have reached us, is also the following verse of Matthew:

And then shall appear the sign of the Son of man in heaven: and then shall all the tribes of the earth mourn, and they shall see the Son of man coming in the clouds of heaven with power and great glory. (Matthew 24:30)

Jesus says that a time will come when, from heaven, as a result of divine intervention, such knowledge and evidence will come to hand as will invalidate the doctrines of his divinity, death on the cross, going up to heaven and coming back again; and that heaven will bear witness against the lies of those, for example the Jews, who denied his being a true prophet, and condemned him as accursed on account of his death on the cross. The fact that he did not suffer death on the cross and was, therefore, not accursed would be clearly established; that as a result all the nations of the earth, who had exaggerated or detracted from his true station, would become greatly ashamed of their error; that, in the same age, when this fact would be disclosed, people would see Jesus' spiritual descent to the earth. It means that the Promised Messiah, who would come in the power and spirit of Jesus, would appear with all the lustrous signs, heavenly support, and power and glory which would be easily recognised. When further explained, the verse means that God's will has so made the person of Jesus and such are the events of his life that they cause some people to exaggerate, and others to downgrade his status. There are those who have placed him above the category of human beings, so much so that they say that he has not yet died and is sitting alive in heaven. Then there are those who have gone one better and say that, having died on the cross and come back to life again, he has gone to heaven and become invested with all the powers of divinity and that he is God Himself. Then there are the Jews, who say that he was killed on the cross and therefore (We take refuge with God for this) he is accursed for all times to come; that he is doomed to be the object of perpetual divine wrath; that God is disgusted with him and looks upon him as his hated enemy; that he is a liar, an impostor, an apostate, and a rank unbeliever and that he is not from God. (We again take refuge with God for this). These exaggerations and detractions were so unjust that it was but natural that God Himself should exonerate His true prophet from these charges. The verse of the Gospel quoted above also points to this fact. The statement that all the nations of the earth would mourn and lament suggests that all those people to whom the term 'nation' applies would mourn on that day; they would beat their breasts and cry, and great would be their mourning. Christians had better study this verse a little carefully and consider. When the verse prophesies that all the nations would beat their breasts, how then is it possible that Christians shall stay away from this mourning? Are they not a nation? When, in accordance with this verse, they are a part of those who shall beat their breasts, why then are they not concerned about their salvation? The verse clearly says that when the sign of the Messiah appears in the heavens, all the nations inhabiting the earth will mourn. Anyone who says that his people will not mourn denies Jesus. Only those who are yet a small minority cannot be the people hinted at in the prophecy, as they are not yet numerous enough to be described as a nation. These people are none but us. Ours is the only community which is outside the sense and scope of this prophecy, for this community has yet only a few adherents to whom the term 'nation' cannot be applied. Jesus, on the authority of divine revelation, says that when a particular sign appears in the heavens all the people of the world who, on account of their numbers, deserve to be described as a nation will beat their breasts; there will be no exception but those who are small in number and to whom the term nation cannot apply. Neither Christians, nor Muslims, nor Jews, nor any other denier, can keep out of the purview of this prophecy. Our community alone is outside its scope for God has only just sowed us like a seed. The word of a prophet can never fail. The prophecy contains the unmistakable hint that every nation inhabiting the world will mourn. Now which of these people can claim to be outside its scope? Jesus admits of no exception in this verse. The group which has not yet attained the size of a nation is in any case an exception, and that is our community. This prophecy has been clearly fulfilled in this age, for the truth, which has now been revealed regarding Jesus, is undoubtedly the cause of mourning for all these nations, because it has exposed the error of their thinking. The hue and cry of Christians over the divinity of Jesus turns into sighs of grief; the insistence of Muslims day in and day out that Jesus has gone up to the skies alive, changes into weeping and wailing; and as for the Jews, they stand to lose everything.

Here it is necessary to mention that in the statement contained in the said verse, namely, that at that time all the nations of the earth would mourn and beat their breasts, the word 'earth' means Bilaad-i-Shaam[17] with which these three peoples are basically connected — Jews, because that is their place of origin and their place of worship; Christians, because Jesus appeared in that place, and the early Christians lived there; Muslims, because they are the heirs to the land to the Last Day. If the word 'earth' is taken to embrace all countries, even then it presents no difficulty, for

---

[17] Syria and its neighbouring areas. (Translator)

when the truth is laid bare all deniers would be ashamed.

Among the testimonies that have reached us through the Gospels, is this statement from the Gospel of Matthew:

> *And the graves were opened; and many bodies of the saints which slept arose, and came out of the graves after his (Jesus') resurrection and went into the holy city, and appeared unto many. (Matthew 27:52)*

There is not the slightest doubt that the story mentioned in the Gospel that after the resurrection of Jesus the saints came out of the graves and appeared alive to many, is not based on any historical fact; for, had it been so, the Judgment Day would have taken place in this very world, and what had been kept secret as a test of faith and sincerity would have been made manifest to all. Faith would not have been faith, and, in the sight of every believer and denier, the nature of the next world would have become an evident and open fact, like the existence of the moon, the sun, and the alternation of day and night. In that case, faith would have no value, nor would it merit any reward.

If the people and past prophets of Israel whose number is millions, had really been brought to life at the time of the crucifixion and had in fact come back to the city alive, and if this miracle, that hundred of thousands of saints and prophets were all brought to life at the same time, were really shown to prove the truth and divinity of Jesus, the Jews would have had an excellent opportunity to inquire of their prophets, saints, and other ancestors, whether Jesus who claimed to be God was indeed God, or was he a liar! One can easily imagine that they could not have missed this welcome opportunity. They must have inquired about Jesus, for the Jews were very keen to compare notes with the dead if they could be restored to life. When, therefore, hundreds of thousands of the dead were restored to life, and flocked to the city in their thousands, how could the Jews have let go such an opportunity? They must have inquired, not from one or two, but from thousands; and when the dead entered their respective houses there must have been great commotion all over the place, for many hundreds of thousands of them had been brought back to life. In every house there must have been great excitement, and everybody must have been questioning the dead as to whether the man Jesus, who called himself the Messiah, was really God. But because the Jews, after the testimony of the dead, did not believe in Jesus, as we would expect them to do, nor did their hearts soften, rather if anything, they became confirmed in their hard-heartedness, it appears more than probable that the dead did not speak a single favourable word for him. They must have pronounced straightaway that this man was making a false claim to Godhood, and was lying against God. That was why the Jews did not desist from mischief in spite of the fact that hundreds of thousands of prophets and apostles had been restored to life. Having 'killed' Jesus, they attempted to kill all others. How can one believe that hundreds of thousands of saints who, right from the time of Adam up to the time of John the Baptist, had been resting in their graves in the holy land, should all be brought back to life; that they should all flock to the city to preach, and everyone of them should stand up and testify before thousands of people that Jesus, the Messiah, was really the Son of God – no, God Himself; that he alone should be worshipped; that the people should renounce their former beliefs, otherwise, they would go to hell, which these saints had witnessed for themselves! Yet, notwithstanding such excellent evidence and such eyewitness accounts which proceeded from the mouths of hundreds of thousands of dead saints, the Jews should not desist from their denial! I personally am not prepared to believe this. Therefore, if hundreds of thousands of saints, prophets and apostles, etc., who were dead, had really come to life and had visited the city to give evidence, they must undoubtedly have given unfavourable evidence; they could never have borne witness to the divinity of Jesus. Perhaps this is the reason why the Jews became more firmly entrenched in their disbelief after listening to the evidence of the dead. Jesus wanted them to believe in his divinity, but they, because of this evidence, denied that he was even a prophet.

In short, such beliefs have a highly deleterious and unhealthy effect, namely, to say that hundreds of thousands of dead persons, or any dead person before that time, had been brought back to life by Jesus; for the restoration to life of the dead did not serve any useful purpose. A person who has visited a far-off country and comes back to his hometown after several years of absence is naturally keen to tell the people of his strange experiences, and to relate to them the wonderful stories of the land he has visited. He will not keep mum or remain tongue-tied when he meets his people after a long period of separation. No, at such a time, others also are keen to listen to him and question him about the far off places; and if perchance, there comes to these people some poor and lowly person, humble in appearance, who yet claims to be the king of the country of which the principal town has already been visited by these people and who says that he is superior in his kingly rank even to this and that king, the people are always wont to question such itinerants whether the man, going about in their country, is really the king of that land; to which question these travellers reply to the best of their knowledge. This being so, the bringing of the dead to life by Jesus would have been, as I have stated before, worth believing in, if the evidence on which the dead must have been questioned, which was but natural, had led to some useful result. However, this was not at all the case. Therefore, along with the supposition that the dead were brought back to life, one is compelled to suppose that the dead did not give evidence favourable to Jesus which could lead one to believe in his truth. They rather gave evidence which added to the already existing confusion. Would that instead of human beings, some animal had been restored to life! Perhaps the idea was to preserve secrecy. For example, if it had been said that Jesus had brought back to life several thousand bullocks, it would have been 'reasonable' enough, and, if the question was asked as to what the evidence of these dead animals had led to, the answer would have been easy: how could the mute bullocks testify one way or the other? The dead, however, whom Jesus brought back to life, were human beings. Suppose some of the Hindus were asked if ten or twenty of their dead ancestors were restored to life and brought back to this world and were asked to state which religion was the true religion, would they still have any doubt about the truth of that religion? They would never say No. Therefore, take it for a certainty that there is no man in the whole world who would persist in his disbelief and denial after such a disclosure. What a pity that

in inventing such stories, the Sikhs of our country have
fared better than the Christians. The Sikhs have given proof
of their astuteness in the art of inventing stories; for they
state that their Guru, Bawa Nanak, once restored a dead
elephant to life. This 'miracle' is not open to the above
objection, for the Sikhs can say: the elephant had no tongue
to bear witness for or against Bawa Nanak. In short, the
common people, endowed with little intellect, are pleased
with such 'miracles', but the wise are embarrassed by the
objections raised by others and are put to shame when such
silly stories are related. Now, as I bear the same feelings of
love and sincerity towards Jesus as do the Christians; rather,
I have a stronger attachment to him, for Christians do not
know the man whom they praise, but I know him whom I
praise, for I have as good as seen him. Therefore, I now
proceed to unveil the real nature of the reports contained in
the Gospels that at the time of the crucifixion all dead saints
had come back to life and returned to the city.

Let it, therefore, be clearly understood that accounts like
these are of the nature of *Kashf* or visions that were seen by
some holy men after the crucifixion, in which they saw that
the dead saints had been brought back to life and graced the
city where they met the people. Just as dreams mentioned in
divine scriptures are interpreted, for instance, Joseph's
dream, this vision too had an interpretation of its own. The
interpretation was that Jesus had not died on the cross and
that God had rescued him. If the question is asked as to the
rationale behind this interpretation, the answer is that
experts in the art of interpretation testify to its validity and
have borne witness to it on the basis of their experience. I
quote below from *T'atirul-Anaam*, a time honoured

authority on the art of interpretation of dreams:

من رأى أن الموتى وثبوا من قبورهم و رجعوا إلى دورهم فانه يطلق من فى السجن

(T'atirul-Anaam fi T'abiril-Manaam by Qutb-uz-Zaman Sheikh Abdul Ghani Al-Naablisi, page 289).

This means that if someone has a dream or a vision that the dead have come out of their graves and have made for their homes, the interpretation is that a prisoner would be released from bondage, and that he would be rescued from the hands of his persecutors. The context shows that this prisoner would be a great and prominent personage. Now, it should be noted how appropriately this interpretation applies to Jesus. One can readily understand that the vision about the dead saints coming to life and returning to the city was meant to inform those with insight that Jesus would be saved from death on the cross.

Likewise, the Gospels at a number of places clearly point out that Jesus did not die on the cross and that he escaped and migrated to another land. I think what I have said so far should suffice for the fair minded to understand the true position. It is possible that objections may arise in some minds that the Gospels also repeatedly point out that Jesus died on the cross, and that after resurrection he rose to heaven. This kind of objection I have already briefly answered, but I might as well repeat that after the crucifixion, Jesus met the disciples; he travelled up to Galilee; ate bread and meat; displayed the wounds on his body; stayed a night with the disciples at Emmaus; escaped secretly from Pilate's jurisdiction; emigrated from that place, as was the practice of prophets; and travelled under the shadow of fear. All these facts prove that he did not die on the cross; that he retained his bodily functions intact; and that he had undergone no visible change.

Furthermore, the Gospels do not contain any eyewitness account of Jesus' ascent to heaven.* Had there been such an account, it would have lacked credibility, for making mountains out of molehills and magnifying small things into big ones, seems to be a habit with the evangelists. For example, if one of them happens to remark that Jesus is the Son of God, another sets about making him into a full-fledged God, the third invests him with power over the whole universe, and the fourth bluntly says that he is everything, and that there is no other God besides him. In short, exaggerations carry them too far. The vision in which the dead were seen to come out of their graves and make for the city is a case in point. One can notice that this vision had been given a literal interpretation, so far as to say that the dead had actually risen out of their graves, had come to the city of Jerusalem, and even visited their relatives. Consider how a mountain has been made out of a molehill, resulting in a veritable range! How can one arrive at the truth when things are so exaggerated! It is also worth considering that the Gospels, the so-called Books of God, contain preposterous claims, such as that if all the works of Jesus had been committed to writing, there wouldn't be room enough in the whole world to accommodate them![18] Can such exaggeration be the way of honesty and truth? If indeed works of Jesus were so limitless and exceeded all

---

* No one testifies that he is an eyewitness and that he saw for himself Jesus' bodily ascent to the heavens. (Author)
18 John 21:25 (Translator)

boundaries, how could they have been compressed into a meager period of three years? Another difficulty about these Gospels is that the references they give of earlier books are mostly wrong; they could not even give Jesus' genealogy correctly. From the Gospels, it appears that the evangelists were rather naive to the extent that they mistook Jesus for a ghost. From the earliest times these Gospels have been open to the charge that they have not been able to preserve the purity of their texts, particularly when there were other books too which were compiled as Gospels. There is no earthly reason why all the statements of those books should be rejected, and why all that is contained in the Gospels, generally so-called, should be admitted as true. We do not think that the other Gospels could contain such unfounded exaggerations as are to be found in the present four Gospels. It is surprising that while on the one hand, they say that Jesus was a righteous person and that his character was without blemish, on the other hand, charges are brought against him as are unworthy of a righteous person. For example, the Israelite prophets, in accordance with the teaching of the Torah, undoubtedly had hundreds of wives each at a time in order that they might thereby produce a whole generation of righteous people. But you will never have heard that any prophet had ever set such an example of permissiveness that he should allow a wanton and lascivious woman, a noted sinner of the city, to touch his body with her hands, to let her rub oil—her sin's earnings—on his head and to stroke his feet with her hair; that he allowed all this to be done by an unchaste young woman, and didn't so much as tell her to stop it. One is saved from giving way to suspicion, which naturally arises on seeing such a spectacle, only by an implicit trust in the goodness of Jesus. Nevertheless, the example is hardly worthy of being followed. In short, these Gospels are full of material which shows that they have not preserved their original form, or that their writers were other than the disciples. For example, can the statement: "And this is well known among the Jews till today"[19] be properly ascribed to Matthew? Does it not show that the writer of the Gospel was some person other than Matthew, who lived at a time when Matthew had already died? Then, the same Gospel of Matthew says:

> *And they were assembled with the elders, and had taken counsel, they gave large money unto the soldiers, Saying, 'Say ye, his disciples came by night and stole him away while we slept. (Matthew 28:12-13)*

It would be noticed how childish and meaningless such statements are. If it means that the Jews wanted to conceal the rising of Jesus from the dead, and had bribed the soldiers so that this great miracle should not become generally known, why was it that Jesus, whose duty it was to proclaim this miracle among the Jews, kept it a secret and forbade even others to disclose it? If it is urged that he was afraid of being caught, I would say, that when the decree of God had descended upon him once and for all, and he had, after suffering death, come to life again, assuming a spiritual body, what fear did he now have of the Jews? Surely, the Jews now had no power over him; he was now beyond and above mortal existence? One observes with regret that while, on the one hand, it is said that he was

---

[19] Matthew 28:15 (Translator)

made to live again and assume a spiritual body, that he met
the disciples and went to Galilee and thence went to
heaven, he was nevertheless afraid of the Jews over quite
trivial things and, in spite of his glorious body, he fled
secretly from the country, lest the Jews should discover him;
he made a journey of 70 *koses* to Galilee in order to save his
life and time and again asked the people not to mention this
to others. Are these the signs and ways of a glorious body?
No, the truth is that his body was neither new nor glorious,
it was the same body with wounds on it, which had been
saved from death; and as there was still the fear of the Jews,
Jesus took all the necessary precautions and left the country.
Anything to the contrary would be senseless and absurd, as
that the Jews had bribed the soldiers to make them say that
the disciples had stolen the corpse while they (the soldiers)
were asleep. If the soldiers were asleep, they could very
well have been asked how on earth they came to know in
their sleep that the corpse of Jesus had been stolen away.
From the mere fact of Jesus not being in the sepulchre, can a
sensible person conclude that he had gone up to heaven?
May there not be other causes as a result of which tombs
might be found empty? At the time of going up to heaven, it
was up to Jesus to meet a few hundred Jews, and also Pilate.
Who was he afraid of in his glorious body? He did not care
to furnish his opponents with the slightest proof. On the
contrary, he took fright and fled to Galilee. That is why we
positively believe that though it is true that he left the
sepulchre, which was a chamber with an opening, and
though it is true that he secretly met the disciples, yet it is
not true that he was given any new and glorious body. It
was the same body, and the same wounds, and there was

the same fear in his heart lest the accursed Jews should arrest him again. Just study closely Matthew 28:7-10. These verses clearly say that the women who were told by someone that Jesus was alive and was going to Galilee, and who were also quietly told that they should inform the disciples, were no doubt pleased to hear this, but they departed with hearts full of fear. They were still afraid lest Jesus might still be caught by some wicked Jew. Verse 9 says, that while these women were on their way to inform the disciples, Jesus met and greeted them. Verse 10 says that Jesus told them not to be afraid of his being caught. He asked them to inform his brethren that they should all go to Galilee;* that they would see him there, i.e., he could not stay there for fear of the enemy. In short, if Jesus had really come to life after his death and had assumed a glorious body, it was up to him to furnish proof of this new kind of existence to the Jews. But we know that he did not do this. It is absurd, therefore, to accuse the Jews of trying to suppress the proof of Jesus' coming to life again. Nor for that matter did Jesus give the slightest proof of his restoration to life; rather, by his secret flight, by the fact of his taking food, and sleep, and showing his wounds, he himself proved that he did not die on the cross.

---

* Here, Jesus did not console the women with the words that he had risen with a new and glorious body and that no one could now lay his hands upon him. Instead, seeing the women weak and frail he consoled them casually, as men are wont to console women. In short, he gave no proof of the glorious body; rather, he exhibited his flesh and bones and thus demonstrated that his was an ordinary mortal body. (Author)

Chapter Two

Containing Evidence from the Holy Quran and Authentic *Ahadith* which Relates to Jesus being Saved from the Cross

The arguments which I am now going to set down might seem to all intents and purposes of little use to the Christians, because they are not bound by what the Holy Quran and the *Hadith* have to say on the subject. But I still mention them because I wish to inform the Christians of a miracle of the Holy Quran and the Holy Prophet[sa]; I want them to know that the truths which have now been discovered after hundreds of years have already been disclosed by our Holy Prophet[sa] and the Holy Quran. I am now going to mention some of them. God says in the Holy Quran:

$$^{20} \text{وَمَا قَتَلُوْهُ وَ مَا صَلَبُوْهُ وَ لٰكِنْ شُبِّهَ لَهُمْ} \ldots \text{وَمَا قَتَلُوْهُ يَقِيْنًا}$$

It means the Jews neither murdered Jesus, nor did they kill him on the cross; they were merely labouring under the misconception that Jesus had died on the cross; they did not have evidence enough to convince and satisfy them that Jesus had really died on the cross.

In these verses God Almighty says that though it is true that Jesus was apparently placed on the cross, and that the intention was to kill him; yet it was wrong for the Jews and Christians to suppose that Jesus actually died on the cross.

---

20 4 : 158 (Translator)

What happened was that God caused things to happen which saved Jesus from death on the cross. Justice demands that we acknowledge the truth of what the Holy Quran has said, as opposed to the Jewish and Christian beliefs. Highly qualified modern researchers have proved that Jesus had actually been saved from death on the cross. A study of the records shows that the Jews have never been able to answer the question as to how Jesus died within two or three hours of being put on the cross even when his bones had not been broken? This has led the Jews to invent another plea: that they killed Jesus by the sword, but the ancient history of the Jews does not show that Jesus was killed by the sword. In order to save Jesus, divine power and majesty intervened and caused darkness to prevail, which was followed by an earthquake. Pilate's wife saw a dream. The Sabbath night during which it was illegal to let a crucified body remain on the cross was drawing close. The magistrate, because of the terrible dream, became disposed towards the release of Jesus. All this was simultaneously brought about by God to save Jesus, and Jesus himself was made to go into a swoon so that he might be taken for dead. Through terrible signs like the earthquake, the Jews panicked and became fearful of heavenly punishment. They were also afraid lest the corpses should remain on their crosses during the night of Sabbath. They thought that Jesus was dead when, in fact, he was in a coma. It was dark and there was an earthquake and great turmoil. They also became anxious about their homes and what their children must be passing through in the darkness and the earthquake. There was terror in their hearts that if this man was a liar and an apostate, as they thought he was, why were mighty signs manifested at the moment of his suffering, signs which had not been manifested before? They were so upset that they were no longer in a position to find out for themselves whether Jesus had really died, or what exactly his condition was? What had come about, however, was a Divine design to save Jesus, to which the verse وَلَـٰكِن شُبِّهَ لَهُمْ that is, *'the Jews did not kill Jesus; but it was God who made them believe that they had killed him,'* refers. It is these circumstances which encourage the righteous to place great trust in God, and to believe that God can save His servants as He pleases.

The Holy Quran also says concerning the Messiah, son of Mary:

$$\text{وَجِيهًا فِى الدُّنْيَا وَ الْاٰخِرَةِ وَ مِنَ الْمُقَرَّبِيْنَ }^{21}$$

This means that not only will Jesus have honour and eminence, and enjoy greatness in the people's eyes in this world, but also in the hereafter. It is evident that Jesus was not honoured in the land of Herod and Pilate. On the contrary, he suffered great disgrace and insult. That he would be honoured during his second coming to this earth is a groundless delusion, which is diametrically opposed to the Scriptures and God's eternal law of nature. The truth is that Jesus, having escaped from those accursed people, graced the land of the Punjab with his presence, where he met the ten lost tribes of Israel and God blessed him with great honour and eminence. It seems that most of them had adopted Buddhism and some had degenerated into idolatry of a very low kind. But with the coming here of Jesus, most of them returned to the right path, and since the teaching of

---

21 3 : 46 (Translator)

Jesus contained the exhortation to believe in the coming of another prophet, all the ten tribes who came to be known in this land as Afghans and Kashmiris ultimately became Muslims. Jesus was accorded great esteem and respect in this land. Recently a coin has been discovered in the Punjab, which bears the name of Jesus in Pali characters. This coin goes back to the time of Jesus, and it clearly shows that he came to this land and was given royal reception, and the coin must have been issued by a king who had become his follower. Another coin displays the figure of an Israelite male. It appears that this too is the figure of Jesus. The Holy Quran also contains a verse which says that Jesus was blessed by God wherever he went.[22] And these coins show that he received great blessings from God, and that he did not die until he was honoured like a king.

Elsewhere the Holy Quran says:

وَ مُطَهِّرُكَ مِنَ الَّذِيْنَ كَفَرُوْا[23]

Meaning that, '0 Jesus! I shall clear thee of these charges; I shall prove thy innocence and shall clear thee of all accusations levelled against thee by the Jews and the Christians.' This was indeed a great prophecy. The Jews alleged that Jesus, having been crucified, became accursed (God forbid), and thus forfeited the love of God, that Jesus' heart, as the word 'curse' applies, was estranged and alienated from God, that his heart became enveloped in a thick veil of darkness, came to love evil and hate virtue, broke away from God and was brought under the sway of

---

[22] وَ جَعَلَنِيْ مُبٰرَكًا اَيْنَ مَا كُنْتُ - 19 : 32 (Translator)
[23] 3 : 56 (Translator)

the Satan and that there was real animosity between him and God! The same charge of his being accursed, was brought by Christians too, who have so naively tried to combine two contradictory views. On the one hand, they say that Jesus was the Son of God, and on the other, they call him accursed. What is more, they admit that one who is accursed is the son of Darkness and of the Devil, rather he is the Devil himself. So, these were the foul charges brought against Jesus. The prophecy of the Holy Quran, however, points out that a time would come when God would clear Jesus of these charges and this indeed is the time when this was to happen.

The testimony of the Holy Prophet[sa] has no doubt established the innocence of Jesus in the eyes of thoughtful people, for the Holy Prophet[sa] and the Holy Quran have both testified that the charges brought against Jesus are all unfounded. But this evidence was too subtle and difficult for the common man to understand. Divine justice, therefore, required that just as the crucifixion of Jesus was a known, objective and tangible event, so should his innocence and exoneration be demonstrated objectively. And this is what has actually come to pass. The innocence of Jesus has not only been proved *a priori* but also *a posteriori*. For hundreds of thousands of people have, with their own eyes, seen that the tomb of Jesus lies in Srinagar,[24] Kashmir. As Jesus was crucified at Golgotha or the site of the Skull, his tomb too has been found at the site of the Skull i.e.

---

[24] The word 'Srinagar' comprises two Hindi words, 'siri' (skull) and 'nagar' (place), meaning 'Place of Skull'. The place where Jesus was put on the cross, was also called 'Place of Skull'. See Matthew 27:33, Mark 15:22, Luke 23:33, John 19:17. (Translator)

Srinagar. That the word *Sri* (Skull) should occur in the names of both the places is a strange coincidence indeed. The place where Jesus was crucified was called Gilgit (Golgotha) or *Sri* (Skull), and the place where in the latter part of the nineteenth century, the tomb of Jesus has been discovered is also called *Gilgit*, or *Sri*. It appears that the place called Gilgit, Kashmir, also suggests the term *Sri*. This town was probably founded in the time of Jesus, and as a local memorial to the crucifixion, it was named Gilgit, or Sri; similarly Lhasa, which means the 'city of one worthy of worship'; is of Hebrew origin, and Lhasa too was founded in the time of Jesus.

Reliable reports in the *Ahadith* show that the Holy Prophet[sa] said that Jesus lived to an advanced age of 125. Besides, all the sects of Islam believe that Jesus had two unique characteristics as are not to be found in any other prophet:

  i. He lived to the ripe old age of 125 years.
 ii. He extensively travelled in many parts of the world and was therefore called the *'travelling prophet'*.

It is evident that had he been raised to the skies at 33, the report that he lived for 125 years could not be true, nor could he have managed to travel so widely when he was a mere 33. Not only is this report found in the old and reliable collections of *Ahadith*, it is not possible to think of a report which is more widely known and so consistently accepted among all the sects of Islam.

Kanz-ul-Ummal, which is a comprehensive collection of *Ahadith*, contains this *Hadith*, in volume 2 page 34, from Abu Huraira[rz]:

اوحی اللّٰه تعالیٰ الی عیسیٰ ان یا عیسیٰ انتقل من مکان الی مکان لئلا تعرف فتوذیٰ25

God revealed to Jesus thus: '0 Jesus! Keep on moving from one place to another', go from one country to another lest thou shouldst be recognised and persecuted.

Again, in the same Book (volume 2 page 71) Jaabir[rz] reports:

کان عیسی ابن مریم یسیح فاذا امسی اکل بقل الصحراء و یشرب ماء القراح 26

Jesus continuously travelled from one country to another, wherever he happened to be at nightfall, he would partake of the vegetables of the jungle and drink fresh water.

And in the same book (volume 6 page 51) Abdullah bin Umar[rz] reports:

قال احب شئ الی اللّٰه الغرباء قیل ای شئ الغرباء قال الذین یفرّون بدینهم و یجتمعون الی عیسی ابن مریم 27

The Holy Prophet[sa] said: 'The people most favoured in the sight of God are the Ghareeb.' When asked, what was meant by the term Ghareeb, he replied 'They are the people who, like Jesus, the Messiah, have to flee from their country to save their faith?'

---

25 See کنز العمال الکتاب الثالث من حرف الهمزة الباب الاول فی الاخلاق و الافعال المحمودة – فصل خوف العاقبة – رقم الحدیث 5955 [Translator]

26 The word یشرب is a misprint. It should be شرب. (See کنز العمال الکتاب الثالث من حرف الهمزة – الباب الاول فی الاخلاق و الافعال المحمودة – فصل الصبر علی انواع البلایا و المکاره – رقم الحدیث 6852) [Translator]

27 See کنز العمال کتاب الفتن من قسم الافعال – فصل فی الوصیة فی الفتن printed at Daira-tul-Maarif Al-Nizamia Press, Hyderabad, India, 1313 Hijra. [Translator]

Chapter Three

Evidence from Medical Literature

We have come across a piece of highly valuable evidence concerning the escape of Jesus from the cross, whose authenticity one just can't help admitting. It is a medical preparation known as *Marham-i-Isa* or the 'Ointment of Jesus' and is found recorded in hundreds of medical books. Some of these books were compiled by Christians, some by Magians or even Jews, and some by Muslims. Most of them are old classics. Investigations show that in the beginning, based on oral tradition, the preparation came to be known by hundreds of thousands of people. Later it was duly recorded. In the days of Jesus, shortly after the crucifixion, a pharmacopoeia was compiled in Latin, which recorded this prescription and testified that it had been prepared for the treatment of the wounds of Jesus. Later, this work was translated into several other languages, until, in the time of Mamun-al-Rashid, it was translated into Arabic. Strange are the ways of divine providence, eminent physicians of all religions, Christians, Jews, Magians and Muslims, have all recorded this preparation in their books, and have admitted that it was prepared for Jesus by the disciples. A study of different pharmacopoeias shows that this preparation is very useful in injuries sustained by blows or falls; it immediately arrests the flow of blood, and, as it contains 'myrrh', the wound remains aseptic. The ointment is also useful in plague; it is good for boils and ulcers of all kinds.

It is, however, not clear whether the ointment was prepared by Jesus himself after he had undergone the trauma of the cross, as a result of divine revelation, or that it was prepared after consultation with some physician. Some of its ingredients are specifics, especially 'myrrh' which is mentioned also in the Torah. In any case, the wounds of Jesus healed up in a few days by the use of this ointment. Within three days he recovered sufficiently to be able to march 70 *Koses* on foot from Jerusalem to Galilee. Hence, regarding the efficacy of this preparation, it is enough to say that while Jesus healed others, this preparation healed Jesus! The books which record this fact number more than one thousand. It would take long to mention them all. Moreover, as the prescription is a famous one among the physicians practising Greek medicine, I need not mention the titles of all these books; but I shall set down below the names of a few which are available here.

List of books containing a mention of Marham-i-Isa, and a statement that the ointment was prepared for Jesus' wounds

o   *Qaanun* by Sheikh-ul-Rais Bu Ali Sina, Vol.III, page 133.

o   *Sharah Al-Qaanun* by Allama Qutb-ud-Din Shiraazi, Vol.III.

o   *Kaamil-us-Sana'ah* by Ali Bin-al-Abbas Al- Majoosi, Vol.II, page 602.

o   *Majmu'ah Al-Baqaa'i* by Mahmud Muhammad Ismail, Mukhatib of Khaqan , known as father of Muhammad Baqaa Khan, Vol.II, page 497.

o   *Tazkirah ul-ul-Albaab*, by Sheikh Daud Al-Zareer Al-Antaaki, page 303.

o   *Qaraabadin-i-Rumi*, compiled about the time of Jesus

and translated in the reign of Maamun al-Rasheed into Arabic—Skin Diseases.

o *Umdat-ul-Muhtaaj* by Ahmad Bin Hasan al-Rasheedi al-Hakeem. In this book, Marham-i-Isa, and other preparations have been noted from a hundred, perhaps more than a hundred books, all these books being in French.

o *Qaraabadeen*, in Persian, by Hakeem Muhammad Akbar Arzaani— Skin Diseases.

o *Shifa-ul-Asqaam*, vol.II, page 230.

o *Mir'at-ush-Shifaa*, by Hakeem Nathu Shah (manuscript) —Skin Diseases.

o *Zakhira-i-Khawarzam Shaahi*—Skin Diseases.

o *Sharah Qaanun Gilaani*, Vol.III.

o *Sharah Qaanun Qarshi*, Vol.III.

o *Qaraabaadeen* by Alwi Khan—Skin Diseases.

o *Ilaaj-ul-Amraadh* by Hakeem Muhammad Sharif Khan, page 893.

o *Qaraabaadeen*, Greek—Skin Diseases.

o *Tuhfat-ul-Mo'mineen*, on the margin of *Makhzan-ul-Adwiyah*, page 713.

o *Muheet fi-Tibb*, page 367.

o *Ikseer-i-A'azam*, Vol. IV, by Hakeem Muhammad A'azam Khan, alias Naazim-i-Jahan, page 331.

o *Qaraabaadeen* Ma'sumi-ul-Masum bin Karim-ud-Din Al-Shustri Shiraazi.

o *Ujaala-i-Naafiah* by Muhammad Sharif Dehlavi, page 410.

o *Tibb-i-Shibri*, otherwise known as Lawami Shibriyyah by Syed Hussain Shibr Kaazimi, page 471.

o *Makhzan-i-Sulaimaani*, translation of *Iksir-i-Arabi*, page

599, by Muhammad Shams-ud-Din of Bahawalpur.

o *Shifaa-ul-Amraadh,* translated by Maulana Al-Hakim Muhammad Noor Karim, 282.

o *Al-Tibb Dara Shaukohi,* by Nur-ud-Din Muhammad Abdul Hakeem, Ain-ul-Mulk Al-Shiraazi, page 360

o Minhaaj-ud-Dukaan bi-Dastoor-ul-Aayaan fi A'amaal wa Tarkib al-Naafiah lil-Abdaan by Aflaatoon-i-Zamaanah and Rais-i-Awaanah Abul-Minaa Ibn Abi Nasr-il-Attaar Al-Israeli AI-Harooni (i.e., Jew), page 86.

o *Zubdat-ul-Tibb,* by Syed-ul-Imam Abu Ibrahim Ismail bin Hasanul-Hussaini AI-Jurjaani, page 182.

o *Tibb-i-Akbar* by Muhammad Akbar Arzaani, page 242.

o *Mizaan-ul-Tibb* by Muhammad Akbar Arzani, page 152.

o *Sadidi*   by   Rais-ul-Mutakallimeen   Imam-ul Mohaqqiqeen Al-Sadidul-Kaazrooni, Vol.II, page 283.

o *Haadi Kabir,* by Ibn-i-Zakariyaa — Skin Diseases.

o *Qaraabaadeen* by Ibn-i-Tilmeez — Skin Diseases.

o *Qaraabaadeen* by lbn-i-Abi Saadiq — Skin Diseases.

These are only token names. Scientists, especially physicians, know it well that earlier on, under Muslim rule, most of these books were used as text books at important centers of learning, where scholars from as far as Europe came to study. It is a fact, and there is not the slightest exaggeration about it, that in every century there have been millions of people who have been acquainted with these books; hundreds of thousands have been studying them intensively from end to end. We can assert with all the emphasis at our command, that not a single person from among the scholars of Europe and Asia has been ignorant of the names of at least some of the books listed above. When

Hispania and Kasmonu and Satlirnem* were seats of learning, Bu Ali Sina's (Avicenna's) *Qaanun*, a great medical classic in which there is set out the prescription of Marham-i-Isa and other books like Shifaa and Ishaaraat and Bisharaat, on science, astronomy, and philosophy, were eagerly studied by the Europeans. Likewise, the original works of scholars like Abu Nasr Faaraabi, Abu Raihaan, Israaeel, Thabit bin Qurrah and Hunain bin Is'haq, etc., and their translations of Greek classics were also used as text books. Translations of their works are still extant in Europe today. As Muslim rulers were keen patrons of medicine, they got good Greek works translated. Khilafat remained vested for a long time in kings who happened to desire expansion of knowledge more than the extension of their dominions, that was why they not only had Greek books translated into Arabic but also invited learned Pundits from India, and got them to translate medical and other books, rewarding them handsomely. One of the greatest debts that seekers of true knowledge owe to them, therefore, is that they got Latin and Greek medical classics translated into Arabic, which contained a mention of the 'Ointment of Jesus', and which displays and records, almost as an epitaph, the fact that the ointment had been prepared for the treatment of Jesus' injuries. When the scholars of Islamic era, such as Thabit bin Qurrah and Hunain bin Is'haaq who, apart from medicine, other natural sciences, philosophy, etc., were also well versed in Greek, translated the Qaraabaadeen (Pharmacopoeia), which contains details

---

* *Hispania* or Andalusia; *Kasmonu* or Kastamonu; *Satrilnem* or Santarem. (Author)

about Marham-i-Isa, they were wise enough to retain the Greek term *Shalikha*,[28] which means 'twelve', without translating it into Arabic, as a reminder that the book was a translation from Greek. That is why the term *Shalikha* still figures out in almost all the books.

It is also worth noting that though old coins are very useful in solving the great secrets of history, ancient books, which have been known to millions of people throughout the centuries, and have been taught as text books at important seats of learning and are still being used, are a thousand times more valuable than coins and inscriptions. For, in the case of coins and inscriptions, the possibility of fraud is always there. The classics which, ever since their compilation, have been known to millions of people and have been preserved and guarded by all nations and are still being guarded, constitute a much more valuable piece of evidence than coins and inscriptions. Can anyone possibly name a coin or inscription which has attained such fame as the *Qaanun* of Bu Ali Sina (Avicenna)? In short, *Marham-i-Isa* — the ointment of Jesus — constitutes a very important testimony for seekers after truth. If it is to be rejected, all historical testimony would lose credibility. Although the number of such books containing a mention of *Marham-i-Isa* is about one thousand or even more, and these books and their authors are known to millions, anyone who does not accept this obvious, clear and strong proof must be allergic

---

[28] According to *Qaanun* of Avicenna (*Al-Qaanun Fi Al-Tibb* by Abu Ali Ibn-e-Sina vol. 3 chapter 4 on ointments), the Ointment of Jesus has also been known as *Marham Dashlikha, Marham-ul-Hawariyyin*, and *Marham-ur-Rusol*, and contains twelve ingredients corresponding to the twelve disciples. (Translator)

to all historical evidence. Can one ignore with impunity such a strong piece of evidence and can one doubt such incontrovertible testimony which has encompassed all Europe and Asia and which is the result of the combined testimony of famous Jewish, Christian, Magian and Muslim philosophers?

Fair-minded scholars! hasten to accept this great testimony. And listen, O Judges, this is too shining a proof to be ignored. Is it not proper for us to seek light from this Truth which is as bright as the sun?

The suggestion that Jesus might have sustained some injuries before the Call or some time later during his ministry, and not as the result of crucifixion, is nothing but an absurd and meaningless tale. It is simply absurd to say that his hands and feet might have been injured through some other cause, that he might have fallen from a roof, and the ointment might have been prepared for the treatment of the injuries he had thus suffered. It is absurd because before the Call there were no disciples and the ointment speaks of the disciples. The term *Shalikha*, which is Greek for twelve, is still there in these books. Before the Call, moreover, Jesus was not considered important enough for the events of his life to be recorded. His ministry lasted only three-and-a-half years, and during this time no accident or injury, except for the trauma of the cross, has been recorded. The onus of proof lies with him who is under the impression that Jesus sustained these injuries in some other way, for the event of the cross, to which we have referred, is a proved and established historical fact; neither the Jews nor the Christians deny it. The idea that Jesus received his injuries through some other cause is also not supported by the annals of any nation. To entertain such an idea means to deviate deliberately from the path of truth. But the evidence we have produced cannot be rejected with such meaningless objections.

These manuscripts are in existence even today and for my part, I too possess an antique hand-written manuscript of *Qaanun* by Bu Ali Sina. Therefore, it would be highly unfair, indeed it would amount to an outright murder of truth to throw away so transparent a proof. Think it over and over again, ponder deeply, these books are still possessed by Jews, Magians, Christians, Arabs, Persians, Greeks, Romans, Germans and the French. They are also to be found in the ancient libraries of Europe and Asia. Is it proper to turn away from a proof, whose luster dazzles denial? If these books had been compiled only by Muslims, and if they had been in the hands of the followers of Islam alone, there might have been those who could have jumped to the conclusion that Muslims had forged these facts and recorded them in their books with a view to attacking the Christian creed. But, in addition to the reasons which I shall give shortly, this impression is baseless, because the Muslims could never be guilty of a forgery of this kind; for, like Christians, Muslims also believe that after the crucifixion, Jesus ascended to heaven. Muslims, moreover, do not believe that Jesus was ever put on the cross or that he received any injuries as a result of crucifixion. How then could they knowingly forge a statement contradicting their own belief? Apart from this, Islam was not in existence at the time when these books on medicine, in Latin and Greek, were compiled and made current among hundreds of thousands of people. These books contained the prescription of the 'Ointment of Jesus' as well as the explanation that this ointment was prepared for Jesus by his disciples. In the context of religion, those people—Jews, Christians, Muslims and Magians – were all opposed to one another. Therefore, the fact that they have mentioned this ointment in their books, regardless of their respective beliefs, proves beyond any doubt that the preparation of the ointment was too well known a fact to be denied by any community or nation. True, until the coming of the Promised Messiah, it did not occur to any of these people to make use of the historical importance of this ointment which was recorded in hundreds of books and was known to millions of people of different nationalities. We have nothing to say here except to acknowledge that God willed it so, and it had been predestined by Him, that this sharp and shining weapon and this crucial and decisive evidence which was meant to destroy the creed of the cross would come to light at the hands of the Promised Messiah. The Holy Prophet[sa] had prophesied that the faith of the cross shall neither decline nor shall its progress slow down until the Promised Messiah appeared in this world. It was at his hands that the 'breaking of the cross' was to be brought about. The point which was meant to be underlined was that in the time of the Promised Messiah, God would create conditions which would lay bare the truth about the crucifixion. The creed of the cross would come to an end and complete its life span, not through war or violence, but exclusively through heavenly causes, in the form of scientific reason and argument. This indeed is the meaning of the *Hadith* reported in *Bukhari* and other authentic collections of *Ahadith*. It was inevitable, therefore, that heaven should withhold such incontrovertible proof and conclusive evidence until the coming of the Promised Messiah. And so has it come to pass. After the appearance of the Promised One, eyes shall open and thinking people shall begin to think, for the Messiah, the Promised One of God has come; minds shall now be illuminated; hearts shall begin to respond; pens shall come alive; people shall pick up courage; the righteous shall now be given insight; and every seeker shall be granted reason. For, whatever shines in heaven must illuminate the earth. Blessed and fortunate is he who has a share of this light. As the fruit ripens in season, so does the light descend at its appointed time. No one can make it descend before it descends of itself, nor can anyone stop it when it does descend. Differences and controversies are always there. In the end, however, truth will prevail, for this is not the work of man; nor has the son of man the power to do it. It is God who changes the seasons, rotates time, and converts night into day and day into night. He creates darkness but loves light. He lets even *Shirk*—polytheistic beliefs—spread in the world, but He loves *Tauhid*—His Unity. He likes His glory to be His and no one else's. Ever since the birth of man, and until he disappears from the world, the divine law has been that God supports His *Tauhid* or Oneness. The object of all the prophets sent by Him was to eradicate the worship of man and of other creatures and to establish the worship of God in the world. Their duty was to make **29** لا إله إلا الله shine in the earth as it shines in heaven. The greatest of them,

---

29 There is no God but Allah. [Translator]

therefore, is he who highlighted this formula with such brilliance; who first exposed the impotence of false gods and proved their insignificance on grounds of reason and strength, and then, when he had proved everything, he left as a symbol of his decisive victory the testament لَا إِلٰهَ إِلَّا اللّٰه مُحَمَّدٌ رَسُوْلُ اللّٰه [30] He did not pronounce لَا إِلٰهَ إِلَّا اللّٰه as an unproved assertion. No, he first proved it, and exposed the errors of false belief and then inviting the attention of the people declared, 'Look, there is no God besides Him who has demolished all your might and shattered your pride.' Thus it was that as the reminder of an established truth, he taught the blessed *Kalima*:

لَا إِلٰهَ إِلَّا اللّٰهُ مُحَمَّدٌ رَسُوْلُ اللّٰهِ

---

[30] There is no God but Allah, Muhammad is the Messenger of Allah. (Translator)

Chapter Four

Evidence found in Historical Records

Since this chapter contains different kinds of evidence, I have, for the sake of clarity, divided it into various sections, as follows:

Section One

Evidence from Islamic Literature concerning Jesus' Journeys

On page 130-135 of *Rauzat-us-Safaa*, a well-known book of history in the Persian language, we find an account which, briefly translated, reads as follows:

> *Jesus was named the Messiah because he was a great traveller. He wore a woolen scarf over his head, and a woolen cloak on his person. Carrying a staff in his hand, he used to wander from country to country and city to city. He slept wherever the night found him. He ate vegetables of the jungle, drank fresh water, and travelled on foot. His companions, in one of his travels, once bought a horse for him; he rode the horse one day, but as he could not make any provision for feeding it, he returned it. Journeying from his country, he arrived at Nasibain, which lay at a distance of several hundred koses from his home. He was accompanied by a few of his disciples whom he sent into the city to preach. In the city, however, false and unfounded rumours were current about Jesus and his mother. The governor of the city, therefore, arrested the disciples and summoned Jesus. Jesus miraculously healed some patients and showed some other miracles. As a result, the king of the territory of Nasibain, with all his armies and his people, became his follower. The incident about the 'coming down of food' mentioned in the Holy Quran took place during his travels.*

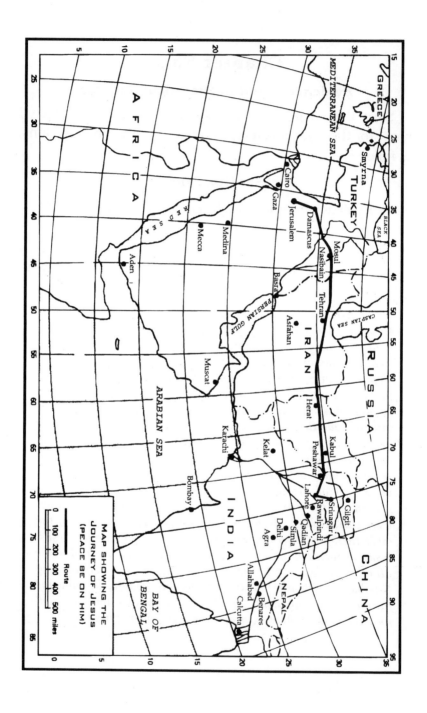

MAP SHOWING THE
JOURNEY OF JESUS
(PEACE BE ON HIM)

—— Route

0 100 200 300 400 500 miles

This, in brief, is the report given in *Rauzat-us-Safaa*. The author of the book, however, has also ascribed many an absurd and irrational miracle to Jesus, which I regret to leave aside, and keeping my account free from falsehood and senseless exaggerations, I turn to the real point at issue which leads to the conclusion that Jesus in the course of his travels, had arrived at Nasibain. Nasibain is a place between Mosul and Syria which, in English maps, has been shown as Nasibus. If one travels from Syria towards Persia, one would pass through Nasibain, which is at a distance of nearly 450 *koses*[31] from Jerusalem. Mosul is nearly 48 miles from Nasibain and 500 miles from Jerusalem. The frontier of Persia lies at a distance of a mere 100 miles from Mosul. This means that Nasibain is 150 miles from the frontier of Persia. The eastern frontier of Persia touches the town of Herat in Afghanistan. Herat lies on the western frontier of Afghanistan in the direction of the Persian territory and is about 900 miles from the western boundary of Persia. From Herat up to the Khyber Pass, the distance measures about 500 miles. The map showing the route followed by Jesus is given here. It shows the route taken by Jesus in his journey to Kashmir. The object of his journey was to meet the Israelites whom the king, Shalmaneser, had taken as captives to Media.[*]

---

[31] This is a misprint in the first edition. It should be 450 miles not *koses*. (Translator)

[*] **Note:** There is a letter in the 14th section of the first chapter of the history in Greek of the 'Creed of Eusebeus', translated by a Londoner, Heinmer by name, in 1650 A.D., which shows that a king, Abgerus by name, invited Jesus from the land beyond the Euphrates, to his court. The letter sent by Abgerus to Jesus, and the reply to it, are full of fabrications and exaggerations. This much, however, seems to be true, that the king having been apprised of the cruelties of the Jews invited Jesus to his

It should be noticed that in the maps published by
Christians, Media is shown towards the south of the Sea of
Khizar (Azov), where today we find Persia. This means that
Media was at any rate a part of the land which today
constitutes Persia. The eastern frontier of Persia is adjacent
to Afghanistan; there the sea is towards the south and the
TurkishEmpire towards the west. If the report in the *Rauzat-
us-Safaa* is correct, it appears that, by travelling to Nasibain,
Jesus intended to go to Afghanistan through Persia, and to
invite to the Truth the lost tribes of Jews who had come to
be known as Afghans.* The word 'Afghan' appears to be of
Hebrew origin; it is a derivative which means 'brave'. It
appears that at the height of their victories, they adopted
this name for themselves.

In short, Jesus came to the Punjab after passing through
Afghanistan, with the ultimate intention of going to
Kashmir after exploring the Punjab and Hindustan. It
should be noted that Chitral and a strip of the Punjab
separate Kashmir from Afghanistan. If one travels from
Afghanistan to Kashmir, through the Punjab, one has to
journey over a distance of 80 *koses* or about 130 miles, and
via Chitral it would be 100 *koses*.[32]

Jesus, however, wisely took the route through

---

court to give him refuge. The king probably believed that he was a true
prophet. (Author)
* In the Torah there was a promise to the Jews, that if they believed in the
'last' prophet, they would, after passing through much suffering, have
their own sovereign kings and rulers. That promise was fulfilled by the
ten tribes of Israel adopting Islam. That is why there have been great
kings among Afghans as well as among Kashmiris. (Author)
[32] 162 miles approximately. (Translator)

Afghanistan, so that the lost tribes of Israel, known as Afghans, might profit from his presence. The eastern frontier of Kashmir touches Tibet. From Kashmir, he could easily go to Tibet. Having come to the Punjab, he had no difficulty in wandering through the important places of Hindustan before going to Kashmir or Tibet. It is, therefore, quite possible, as some old historical records of this country bear out, that Jesus may have been to Nepal, Benares, and other places. He then must have gone to Kashmir through Jammu or Rawalpindi. As he belonged to a cold country, it is certain that he stayed in these parts only through the winter, and, by the end of March or the beginning of April, must have set out for Kashmir. As Kashmir resembles Shaam,[33] he must have taken up permanent residence in this land. It is also possible that he may have stayed for some time in Afghanistan and it is not improbable that he may even have married there. Since one of the tribes of Afghans is known as *Isa Khel*,[34] it would not be surprising if they were descendants of Jesus. It is to be regretted, however, that the history of Afghanistan is in a confused state. It is, therefore, difficult to arrive at anything definite by studying their tribal chronicles. There is no doubt, however, that the Afghans are Israelites, like the Kashmiris. Those who have taken a contrary view in their writings have been misled in the extreme; they do not seem to have studied the matter closely. The Afghans admit that they are the descendants of Qais and that Qais belongs to the house of Israel. It is, however, not necessary to elaborate the point

---

[33] Syria and its neighbouring areas (Translator)
[34] After the name of Jesus (Isa). (Translator)

here. I have already dealt with this question at length in one
of my books. Here, I am describing the journey of Jesus
through Nasibain, Afghanistan, the Punjab and on to
Kashmir and Tibet. It was on account of this long journey
that he was named 'the travelling prophet', or even 'the
leader of travellers.' A Muslim savant, Arif Billah Abi Bakr
Muhammad bin Muhammad Ibn-ul-Walid Al-Fahri Al-Tar-
tooshi Al-Maaliki, who is renowned for his learning, states
about Jesus, on page 6 of his book *Siraaj-ul-Muluk*,
published by the Khairiyah Press of Egypt in 1306 A.H.:

أين عيسى روح الله و كلمته رأس الزاهدين و إمام السائحين

*Where is Isa, the Ruhullah, and the Kalimatullah, the leader
of the righteous, and chief of travellers?*

This means that Jesus was dead, and that even a great
man like him had departed from this world. It should be
noted that this learned authority calls Jesus not merely '*a
traveller*' but '*the chief of travellers*'.

Likewise, on page 431 of *Lisaan-ul-Arab* it is stated:

قيل سمي عيسى .بمسيح لأنه كان سائحا فى الأرض لا يستقر

*Jesus was named 'Messiah', because he travelled about, and
did not stay at one place.*

The same is recorded in *Taajul-Urus Sharah Qaamus*. Therein
it is also stated that the Messiah is one who has been blessed
with innate righteousness and piety, so much so that even
his touch is blessed and that God gave this name to Jesus
because He gives it to whomsoever He pleases. Opposed to
him is the so-called Messiah who is tainted with evil and
accursedness. He is innately evil and accursed. His very
touch results in evil, sinfulness, and imprecation. This name
was, therefore, given to *Dajjal*, the Antichrist and to all those

who are like him. The two names, Messiah the Traveller and Messiah the Blessed, are not antagonistic to each other. One does not invalidate the other. For, it is a divine practice that God names a man in more than one way and all such names rightly apply to him. In short, Jesus being a traveller has been so well proved by Islamic history that if all the references were copied from those books, I am afraid they would run into a huge tome. What I have stated, therefore, should suffice.

Section Two

Evidence from Buddhist Records

Let it be clear that Buddhist Scriptures have made available to us various kinds of evidence, which, on the whole, is enough to prove that Jesus must have visited the Punjab, Kashmir, and other places. I have set down this evidence, so that all impartial readers may first study it, and then, by arranging it as a connected account in their minds, arrive at the aforesaid conclusion on their own. Here is the evidence. First: the titles given to the Buddha are similar to the titles given to Jesus. Likewise, the events of the life of Buddha resemble those of the life of Jesus. The reference here, however, is to the Buddhism of the areas within the boundaries of Tibet, like Leh, Lhasa, Gilgit and Hams, about which it is proved that they were visited by Jesus. With reference to the similarity of titles, it is enough to point out, that if, for example, Jesus calls himself the Light in his teachings, so has Gautama been called the Buddha in the Buddhistic literature which in Sanskrit means 'Light'. If Jesus has been called the Master in the Gospels, so has the

Buddha been called Saasta or the Master. If Jesus has been called Blessed in the Gospels, so has the Buddha been named Sugt – the Blessed. If Jesus has been called Prince, so has the Buddha been called Prince. Jesus has also been described in the Gospels as one who fulfils the object of his coming, so has the Buddha been called in Buddhistic Scriptures Siddhartha – one who fulfils the object of his coming. Jesus has also been called by the Gospels the refuge of the tired and the weary, so has the Buddha in Buddhistic Scriptures been called Asarn Sarn – the refuge of the refuge-less. Jesus has also been called by the Gospels King, though he said that his was the kingdom of Heaven, so also has the Buddha been called the King. The similarity of events pertaining to both is also proved by events. Just as Jesus was tempted by the Devil with the riches and kingdoms of the world provided he made obeisance to him, so was Buddha tempted when the Devil said to him that he would give him the pomp and splendour of kings if he abandoned the austerity of his living and returned home. But, just as Jesus did not obey the Devil, so, it is recorded, the Buddha too did not obey him.[35] See *Buddhism* by T. W. Rhys Davids and *Buddhism* by Sir Monier Williams.*

This shows that the same titles which Jesus ascribes to himself in the Gospels, have been ascribed to the Buddha in Buddhistic Scriptures which were compiled much later; and just as Jesus was tempted by the Devil, so do these books claim that the Buddha was also tempted by the Devil;

---

[35] See Appendix, extracts 1,2,3,4,5 (Translator)
* See *Chinese Buddhism* by Edkins, *Buddha* by Oldenberg translated by W. Hoey; *Life of Buddha* translated by Rockhill. (Author)

rather, the account of the temptation of the Buddha, as stated in these books, is even longer than the account of the temptation of Jesus. It is recorded that when the Devil offered him the temptation of wealth and kingly honour, the Buddha felt inclined to return home. He, nevertheless, did not succumb to the temptation. But the same Devil met him again one night, bringing with him all his progeny, and tried to frighten him by assuming frightfully grotesque shapes. To the Buddha, these Devils appeared like snakes which were emitting fire from their mouths. The snakes began to throw poison and fire at him but the poison turned into flowers and the fire formed a halo round the Buddha.

The Devil, not having succeeded so far, called upon sixteen of his daughters, and asked them to reveal their beauty to the Buddha who remained totally unmoved; and the Devil was baulked in his designs. He adopted a variety of other tricks, but was helpless against the steadfastness of the Buddha, who continued to rise higher and higher to different stages of spiritual eminence, and, after a long night, that is, after severe and protracted trials, he overcame his enemy, the Devil. The Light of True Knowledge dawned upon him and, with the break of day, as soon as his trials were over, he came to know all. The day this great battle ended was the day of the birth of Buddhism. Gautama was 35 years old at the time when he was called the Buddha[36] or the Light, and the Tree under which he was sitting at the time came to be known as the Tree of Light. Now, if you read the Gospels, you will find how closely the temptation of the Buddha resembles the temptation of Jesus to the

---

[36] See Appendix, extract 2. (Translator)

extent that the Buddha's age at the time was nearly the same as Jesus'. As it appears from Buddhist literature, the Devil did not appear to the Buddha in a corporeal and personified form. It was only a vision seen by the Buddha and the talk of the Devil was a satanic inspiration. The Devil, as he appeared to him, suggested to the Buddha that he should abandon his course and follow him and that if he did so, he would give him all the wealth of the world. Likewise, Christian scholars believe that the Devil who appeared to Jesus did not come to him in any corporeal form, like a human being, before the very eyes of the Jews, traversing the streets in his physical body and talking to Jesus so as to be audible to those present. On the contrary, the meeting was of the nature of a vision seen only by Jesus. The talk too was a kind of inspiration. As is the Devil's old wont, he put his evil intentions into Jesus' heart, which Jesus did not accept, and, like the Buddha, rejected all the Devil's temptations.

The question now arises as to why there was so much resemblance between the Buddha and Jesus. The Aryas in this connection say that Jesus, God forbid, became acquainted with Buddhism in the course of his journeys in India, and having acquired knowledge of the facts of Buddha's life, incorporated them in the Gospel on return to his native country; that Jesus composed his moral precepts by plagiarizing the moral teaching of the Buddha, and that just as the Buddha called himself the Light and Knowledge and adopted other titles, so did Jesus assume all such titles, so much so, that, even the long story of the Temptation of the Buddha was appropriated by him. This, however, is no more than a dishonest fabrication by the Aryas. It is quite untrue that Jesus came to India before the event of the cross, for he did not need to undertake such a journey at the time. The need for it arose only after the Jews of Judea had rejected him and, as far as they were concerned, crucified him. He had, however, been saved by a subtle divine intervention. Jesus felt that he had done his duty in conveying the message to the Jews of that country, and that they did not deserve compassion anymore. Then, on being informed by God that the ten tribes of the Jews had migrated towards India, Jesus set out for those regions. As some of the Jews had accepted Buddhism, there was no alternative for this true prophet but to turn his attention to the followers of Buddhism. As the Buddhist priests of that country were waiting for the 'Messiah Buddha' to appear, they hailed Jesus as the Buddha considering all the signs like his titles, his moral teachings like 'love thine enemy' and 'do not resist evil,' and the Buddha's prophecy about fair skin. It is also possible that some of the titles and teachings and facts of Jesus' life may, consciously or unconsciously, have at that time been ascribed to the Buddha; for the early Indians never had any scruples about recording history objectively. The events of Buddha's life had not been recorded till the time of Jesus. Buddhist priests, therefore, had ample room to ascribe to the Buddha anything they wished. It is quite likely, therefore, that when they came to know of the facts of Jesus' life and his moral teaching, they mixed them up with many of their own innovations and ascribed them to the Buddha.* Presently I

---

* We cannot deny that the Buddhistic faith, from ancient times, has contained a large portion of moral teaching; but at the same time we

shall prove that the part of the moral teaching of Buddhism which resembles that of the Gospels, the titles like 'Light', which are attributed to the Buddha as they are to Jesus, and the Satanic temptations, are all details which were incorporated into the Buddhistic literature only after Jesus' visit to this country which took place after the crucifixion.

There is yet another resemblance between the Buddha and Jesus. Buddhist chronicles show that the Buddha during the temptation was fasting and that the fast lasted for forty days. Readers of the Gospels know that Jesus also observed a forty-day fast.

Anyone who is acquainted with the teachings of Buddha and Jesus will also marvel at the close resemblance and similarity between the moral teaching of the two. For example, the Gospels say, do not resist evil, love your enemy, live in poverty, and shun pride, falsehood and greed; the same is the teaching of the Buddha. Rather the Buddhistic teaching lays greater stress on it, so much so that the killing even of ants and insects has been considered a sin. The outstanding principle of Buddhism is sympathy for the whole world, seeking the welfare of the whole of humanity and of all the animals, and promotion of a spirit of unity and mutual love. The same is the teaching of the Gospels. Again, just as Jesus sent his disciples to different countries, journeying to one himself, so was the case with the Buddha. *Buddhism* by Sir Monier Williams[37] records that

maintain that that part which is merely the teaching of the Gospels — the parables and other reproductions from the Bible -was undoubtedly added to the Buddhistic books at the time Jesus was in this country. (Author)

[37] See Appendix, extract 2. (Translator)

the Buddha sent out his disciples to preach, addressing
them thus: 'Go forth and wander everywhere out of
compassion for the world and for the service of gods and
men. Go forth in different directions, go and preach total
abstinence, piety and celibacy.' He said that he too would
go and preach the same doctrine. Accordingly, the Buddha
went to Benares and worked a number of miracles in that
area. He delivered an impressive sermon on a hill just as
Jesus had delivered his sermon on the mount. Again, the
same book states that the Buddha preached mostly in
parables; he used to explain spiritual phenomena in
material terms.

Let it be remembered that this moral teaching and this
mode of preaching — talking in parables — was the method
of Jesus. This mode of preaching and this moral teaching,
combined with other circumstantial evidence, at once
suggest that all this was in imitation of Jesus. Jesus was here
in India where he preached extensively. The followers of the
Buddhist faith met him, and found him to be a holy and
blessed man. They recorded these things in their books and
even called him the Buddha, for it is part of human nature
to try to acquire a good thing wherever one can find it.
People try to record and remember any clever remark made
by anyone they meet. It is, therefore, quite likely that the
followers of the Buddhist Faith may have reproduced the
entire picture of the Gospels in their books, as, for example,
fasting for forty days both by Jesus and the Buddha; the
Satanic temptation faced by both; the birth of both being
without father; the moral teaching of both; each calling
himself the Light; each calling himself Master and his
companions disciples. Just as Matthew, chapter 10 verses 8

and 9, states: 'Provide neither gold, nor silver, nor brass in your purses,' so did the Buddha command his disciples.[38] Just as the Gospels encourage celibacy, so does the teaching of the Buddha. Just as there was an earthquake after Jesus was put on the cross, so it is recorded, there was an earthquake at the death of the Buddha.[*39] All these points of resemblance arise from the basic fact of Jesus' visit to India. It was indeed a blessing for the followers of the Buddhist faith that he stayed among them for quite some time and they came to have a good knowledge of the facts of his life and of his noble teaching. It was, therefore, inevitable that a great part of his teaching and ceremonial rites should find way into Buddhist records because Jesus was held in great esteem by the Buddhists who had even pronounced him to be the Buddha. That is why they recorded his sayings in their books and ascribed them to Gautama Buddha.

Strangely enough, the Buddha, quite like Jesus, taught his disciples in parables, especially the ones contained in the Gospels. In one of these parables the Buddha says, "As the peasant sows the seed but cannot say the grain shall swell today or germinate tomorrow, so also is it with the disciple. He can't tell if he will germinate well or will be like the grain which is sown in rocky soil and dries up."

This, it will be noted, is the same parable which is still there in the Gospels. The Buddha, again, employed the parable: When a herd of deer prospers in a forest a man comes who opens for them a false path which leads to their death,

---

[38] See Appendix, extract 2. (Translator)
[*] Buddhists also have a tradition similar to the Lord's Supper of the Christians. (Author)
[39] See Appendix, extract 1,2,3,4. (Translator)

that is to say he tries to lead them to a path which ultimately ensnares them brings them to death. And another comes who opens a safe path, that is to say he sows a field from which they can eat and he brings to them a canal so that they may drink thrive; such is the case with men who live in prosperity, the devil comes and opens the eightfold path of evil, so that they may perish. Then comes the Perfect Man and opens the eightfold path of truth, certainty, and peace, so that they will be saved.

The Buddha also taught that the righteousness is a safe treasure which no one can steal. It is a treasure which accompanies man even after death; it is a treasure which is the source of all Knowledge and all Perfection.

It should also be noted that this exactly is the teaching of the Gospels. It is also found in the ancient Buddhist books which belong to the period which is not much different from the time of Jesus; in fact it is the same period. Again, on page 135 of the same book, Buddha is reported to have said that he is so irreproachable that no one can point out a single blot on his character.[40] This too has a close resemblance to a saying of Jesus. *Buddhism*, on page 45, states: "The moral teaching of the Buddha has a striking resemblance with the Christian moral teaching."

I agree with this, and I also agree that both teachings tell us: Love not the world nor wealth; do not hate your enemies; do no evil; conquer evil with good; do to others as you wish to be done by them. All this shows so striking a resemblance between the Gospels and the teaching of the Buddha that it is unnecessary to go into any more detail.

---

[40] See Appendix, extract 2. (Translator)

Buddhistic records also show that Gautama Buddha prophesied the coming of a second Buddha who would be named Metteyya. This prophecy is contained in *Laggavatti Suttatta*,[41] a Buddhist record to which reference is made on page 142 of Oldenberg's book. The prophecy reads thus:

He will be the leader of a band of disciples numbering hundreds of thousands, as I am now the leader of bands of disciples, numbering hundreds.[42]

It may be noticed here that the Hebrew word, Mashiha, is the same as the Pali, Metteyya. It is a matter of common knowledge that when a word is transferred from one language to another, it very often undergoes a phonetic change. An English word, too, when imported into another language, undergoes change: for example, Max Muller, in a list given on page 318 of Volume 11 of *Sacred Books of the East*, says: the *th* of the English alphabet becomes *s* in Persian or Arabic. Keeping these changes in view, one can readily understand that the word Messiah became Metteyya in the Pali language, which means that the future Metteyya prophesied by the Buddha is in reality the Messiah and no one else. This view is supported by the strong evidence of Buddha's own prophecy that the Faith he had founded would not endure in the world for more than five hundred years; that at the time of the decline of the faith and its teachings, the Metteyya would come to this land and re-establish the faith and its teachings in the world. Now we find that Jesus appeared five hundred years after the

---

[41] According to Oldenberg it is spelled *Cakkavatti Suttanta*. See Appendix, extract 5. (Translator)
[42] See Appendix, extract 5. (Translator)

Buddha, and that just as the Buddha had fixed the time frame for the decline of his Faith, Buddhism did indeed deteriorate into a state of decadence as foretold. It was then that, having escaped from the cross, Jesus travelled to those parts, where the Buddhists recognised him readily and treated him with great reverence. There is no doubt that the moral teaching and spiritual exercises taught by the Buddha were resuscitated by Jesus. Christian historians admit that the Sermon on the Mount as reported in the Gospels and the rest of his moral teachings are the same as those preached to the world by the Buddha five hundred years before. They also state that the Buddha not only taught moral precepts, he also taught other great truths. In their view, the title of 'the Light of Asia' applied to the Buddha is highly appropriate. Now, in accordance with the prophecy of the Buddha, Jesus appeared five hundred years after him, and as admitted by most Christian scholars, his teaching was the same as the teaching of the Buddha. There is no doubt, therefore, that he appeared in the 'spirit' of the Buddha. In Oldenberg's book, on the authority of *Lakkavatti Suttatta*,[43] it is stated that the followers of the Buddha, looking forward to his future coming, were sustained by the hope that as disciples of the Metteyya, they would have the bliss of salvation. They were certain that the Metteyya would come and that they would attain salvation through him, for, the words in which the Buddha had held out the hope for the coming of the Metteyya positively showed that his disciples would meet and acknowledge him. The statement of the

---

[43] According to Oldenberg it is spelled *Cakkavatti Suttanta*. See Appendix, extract 5. (Translator)

above-mentioned book further reinforces the conviction that for the guidance of those people God had created two appropriate circumstances: Firstly, by virtue of the title Asif, mentioned in Genesis 3:10,[44] which means 'one who rallies a people', it was inevitable that Jesus should visit the land to which the Jews had migrated and settled; secondly, in accordance with the prophecy of the Buddha, it was necessary that the followers of the Buddha should meet Jesus and profit from him spiritually. Considering both these points together, it looks almost certain that Jesus must have visited Tibet. The fact that Christian teaching and ritual have so deeply influenced Tibetan Buddhism necessitates the belief that Jesus must have visited the Tibetan people also. Moreover, the fact that the zealous followers of Buddhism, as stated in Buddhistic records, had always eagerly expected to meet him, cries out aloud that this desire on their part had become the prelude to Jesus' visit to this country. In the face of both these facts, an impartial person has no need to search through Buddhistic records to discover for himself the statement that Jesus did in fact come to Tibet. For, in accordance with the prophecy of the Buddha, the desire for the Buddha's second advent being so strong, the prophecy itself must have attracted Jesus to Tibet. It must be noted that the word 'Metteyya' so frequently mentioned in Buddhistic books undoubtedly means 'Messiah'. On page 14 of the book, *Tibet, Tartary, Mongolia,* by H. T. Prinsep, it is stated concerning Metteya Buddha, which in reality is Messiah, that the first Christian

---

[44] The sense of the quotation is correct but it seems there is a misprint in the first edition. Please read 49:10 instead of 3:10 (Translator)

missionaries, having heard and seen at first hand conditions obtaining in Tibet, came to the conclusion that in the ancient books of the Lamas there were to be found traces of the Christian religion. Again, on the same page, it is stated that there is no doubt about it that these ancient authorities believed that the disciples of Jesus were still alive when the Christian teaching reached this place. On page 171 it is stated that there is not the slightest doubt that at that time everybody was eagerly waiting for the great Saviour to appear. Tacitus says that it was not only the Jews who were responsible for this belief, but Buddhism itself had laid the foundation for it, i.e., it prophesied the coming of the Metteya. Furthermore, the author of this English work says in a note: The books *Pitakattayan* and *Attha-Katha* contain the clear prophecy concerning the appearance of yet another Buddha, whose advent would take place a thousand years after the time of Gautama or 'Sakhiya Muni'. Gautama himself states, that he is the 25th Buddha and that the 'Bagwa Metteyya' is still to appear, that is, after he has gone, one whose name will be Metteyya who will be fair-skinned will come. The English author goes on to say that the word Metteyya has a striking resemblance to Messiah.[45] In short, Gautama Buddha clearly states in this prophecy that there would arise a Messiah in *his* country, among *his* people and *his* followers. That is why the followers of Buddhism had all the time been waiting for the Messiah to appear in their country. The Buddha, in his prophecy, mentioned him as 'Bagwa Metteyya' because 'Bagwa' in Sanskrit means 'white', and Jesus, being an inhabitant of the Syrian

---

[45] See Appendix, extract 6 (Translator)

territory, was fair-skinned. The people of the land where this prophecy was announced, i.e., the people of Magadh, in which was located Rajagriha, were dark-skinned. Gautama Buddha himself was dark. He had narrated to his followers two conclusive signs regarding the future Buddha.

i. He would be 'Bagwa' or of fair skin.

ii. He would be 'Metteyya', a traveller, and that he would come from a foreign land.

People, therefore, constantly looked out for these signs till they actually saw Jesus. Every Buddhist must necessarily profess the belief that five hundred years after the Buddha, the Bagwa Metteyya did, in fact, appear in their land.* It should not be surprising, therefore, if books of the Buddhist faith should mention the coming of the Metteyya—the Masiha—to their land, and of the fulfilment of Buddha's prophecy. Supposing there is no such mention, even then, because on the basis of divine revelation, the Buddha had communicated to his disciples the tiding that the Bagwa Metteyya would come to their land, no Buddhist who was cognizant of this prophecy could deny the coming to this land of the Bagwa Metteyya, whose other name was Masiha; because the non-fulfillment of the prophecy would have meant the falsity of the faith itself. If this prophecy, for whose fulfilment a time frame had been fixed, and which Gautama Buddha had communicated to his disciples again and again, had not been fulfilled at its appointed time, his followers would have begun to doubt the truth of his claim that he was the Buddha. Also, it would have been placed on

---

* The period of a thousand or five thousand years is incorrect. (Author)

record that this prophecy had not been fulfilled. Another argument in support of the fulfilment of this prophecy is that books belonging to the seventh century A.D. were discovered in Tibet, in which the word 'Mashih' figures out prominently, which means Jesus[as], and it is written as Mi-Shi-Hu. The compiler of the list which contained the word Mi-Shi-Ho is a Buddhist. (Vide *A record of the Buddhist Religion* by I. Tsing, translated by G. Takakusu.) This Takakusu is a Japanese who has translated I. Tsing's book, and I. Tsing is a Chinese traveller. On the margin and in the appendix to the book Takakusu states that an ancient book contains the name Mi-Shi-Ho[46] (Masih). This book belongs approximately to the seventh century....... It was recently translated by the Japanese, G. Takakusu,[*] published by Clarendon Press, Oxford. The book in any case contains the word Mashih which shows with certainty that this word was not imported by the Buddhists from outside; rather, it was borrowed from the prophecy of the Buddha and was written sometimes as Mashih and sometimes as Bagwa Metteyya.

Apart from the testimonies, we have found in Buddhistic chronicles, there is one recorded by Sir Monier Williams, on page 45 of his book *Buddhism*. He says that the sixth disciple of the Buddha was a man named 'Yasa'.[47] The name is Yasu or Yasa for short. As Jesus appeared five hundred years after the death of the Buddha, sometime in the sixth century, he was called the sixth disciple. It should be noted

---

[46] See Appendix, extract 7 (Translator)
[*] See pages 169 and 223 of this book. (Author)
[47] See Appendix, extract 2. (Translator)

that Professor Max Muller, on page 517 of the October 1894 issue of his periodical *The Nineteenth Century,* supports the aforesaid statement and says that established and renowned writers have pointed out many a time that Jesus was influenced by the principles of Buddhism and that attempts are being made even today to discover some historical route along which the principles of the Buddha's faith could be proved to have reached Palestine in the days of Jesus.[48] This observation by Max Muller corroborates the Buddhistic records in which it is claimed in as many words that Yasa was the disciple of the Buddha. When Christians of such repute as Professor Max Muller admit that the principles of Buddhism had certainly influenced Jesus, it would not be far wrong to say that this would amount to his being a disciple of the Buddha. Nevertheless, we consider the use of such a title in respect of Jesus disrespectful and impertinent. The statement found in the Buddhist literature that Yasu was the disciple of the Buddha, is only an example of the age-old habit of Buddhist priests to designate a great personage appearing at a later date as if he were the disciple of his prototype. Apart from this, as has been pointed out, there being great resemblance between the teachings of Jesus and those of the Buddha, it would not be wrong to speak of their relationship as that of the master and the disciple, though such thinking is very irreverent. Nevertheless, we do not approve of the way the European investigators are eager to prove that the teachings of Buddhism had reached Palestine in the days of Jesus. It is, indeed, unfortunate that when the name and mention of

---

[48] See Appendix, extract 8. (Translator)

Jesus are found in the ancient books of Buddhism, these investigators should adopt the dubious course of trying to find traces of Buddha's faith in Palestine. Why should they not search for the blessed footprints of Jesus on the rocky soil of Nepal, Tibet, and Kashmir? I know, however, that these researchers could never be expected to uncover the truth which was lying hidden under a thousand veils of darkness; it was for God to do it. He watched from on high that man-worship was running rampant the world over, and worship of the cross and the supposed sacrifice of a human being had alienated the hearts of millions of people from the true God. In His indignation, He sent to the world his servant in the spirit of Jesus of Nazareth, to demolish the creed of the cross.   And he did come as the Promised Messiah in accordance with the old prophecies. Then at long last came the time for the breaking of the cross, the time when the error of the creed of the cross was to be exposed beyond any doubt quite like a piece of wood torn asunder. Heaven has now thrown open the way for the demolition of the cross, so that the seeker after truth may look around and investigate. True, the physical ascension of Jesus to heaven was a misnomer; nevertheless, it had a significance of its own. The truth about the life of the Messiah had been forgotten and lost, as a corpse is eaten up by the earth and is no more; but in heaven he had an existence of his own and was present like a disembodied human spirit. It was inevitable, therefore, that this reality should finally descend to the earth in the latter days and assume the form of a living human being. This Messianic reality has indeed descended to the earth in this age in the shape of a living human being. It has broken the cross and dispelled the evils of falsehood and its worship. The Holy Prophet^{sa} in a *Hadith* about the cross has compared these evils to the swine. They have now been killed just as swine are killed. It is wrong to interpret this *Hadith* to mean that the Promised Messiah would kill the infidels and break crosses. In reality, the breaking of the cross means that at the time, God of Heaven and Earth would reveal the hidden Truth and, all of a sudden, the entire structure of the cross would collapse. The killing of swine does not mean the killing of men or of swine, but the killing of swinish qualities like persistent falsehood and flaunting it with impunity, which is like eating excrement. Just as dead swine cannot eat dirt, so, there would come a time — in fact, it has already come — when evil would be prevented from gorging on this kind of dirt. Muslim clerics, the *Ulama*, have been grossly mistaken in the interpretation of this prophecy of the Holy Prophet^{sa}. The true meaning of the breaking of the cross and of the killing of the swine are the ones we have already mentioned. If the *Mahdi* and the Messiah were supposed to go on a killing spree, what will become of the other prophecy which says that at the time of the Promised Messiah, religious wars will be brought to an end and Heaven will radiate such resplendent truths as will clearly differentiate between right and wrong. Do not think, therefore, that I have come to wield the sword. No, I have come to put all swords back into their sheaths. The world has been groping in the dark for far too long. Many have conspired against their well-wishers, wounded the hearts of true friends, and hurt their dear ones. But now darkness shall be no more. Night is gone and the day has dawned. Blessed is he who remains not deprived any more!

Among the testimonies contained in Buddhist records is the evidence mentioned on page 419 of *Buddhism* by Oldenberg. It is recorded on the authority of the book named *Mahavagga* (page 54 section 1) that a man called Rahulta[49] was a successor to the Buddha. This Rahulta has been described not only as his devoted disciple, but also as his son. I am convinced that Rahulta of Buddhistic records is none other than Ruhullah, which is one of Jesus' titles and reads as Rahulta due to phonetic variation. To say that Rahulta was the son of the Buddha, who abandoned his child in infancy, went into exile and, wishing to part from his wife for good, left her asleep without informing her or saying farewell, and fled to some other land, is altogether absurd and derogatory to the high spiritual station of the Buddha. It portrays him as a cruel and hard-hearted man who had no compassion for his poor wife and left her asleep and slunk away like a thief without saying a word of consolation to her. He altogether ignored the duties he owed to her as a husband, neither divorcing her nor asking her permission to proceed on an endless journey, wounded her heart by disappearing so suddenly and did not care to send her even a single letter and took no pity on his child who grew up to manhood in his absence. Could such a man, who had no respect for the morals he taught his disciples, be righteous? Conscience refuses to accept this story, just as it refuses to accept the story of the Gospels that once Jesus failed to show regard for his mother, that he did not attend to her when she called on him and uttered words which were disrespectful.

---

[49] Also known as Rahula. See Appendix, extract 5. (Translator)

So although the two stories about hurting the feelings of a wife and a mother have a mutual resemblance, yet we cannot ascribe such stories as do not size up to the lowest level of moral conduct either to Jesus or to Gautama Buddha. If the Buddha loved not his wife, had he no pity on a poor woman and her suffering child either? It is so serious a lapse of moral conduct that I am shocked even to think of this story which is hundreds of years old and belongs to the dead past. Why at all should he have misbehaved like this? To be a bad man, it is enough to be callous towards one's wife, unless she be immoral, disobedient, faithless, or hostile to her husband. We cannot, therefore, ascribe such offensive behaviour to the Buddha, which militates against his own teachings. All this shows that the story is false. In point of fact, 'Rahulta' means Jesus, whose other name is 'Ruhullah'. The word 'Ruhullah' in Hebrew comes close to Rahulta, and 'Rahula', or, 'Ruhullah', has been described as a disciple of the Buddha because, as I have already stated, that Jesus came after the Buddha and brought a dispensation similar to that of the Buddha. That is why the followers of the Buddhist faith declared that the Buddha was the source of the teachings of Jesus, and that Jesus was one of his disciples. It should not be surprising if the Buddha, on the basis of revelation from God, should have declared Jesus to be his 'son'. Another important piece of circumstantial evidence is that in the same book it is recorded that when the infant Rahulta was separated from his mother, a woman whose name was Magdaliyana, and who was a follower of the Buddha acted as the intermediary. It may be noted that the name Magdaliyana is in reality a corrupt form of the name Magdalena, a female follower of Jesus mentioned in the Gospels.

All this evidence, which has been briefly given, should lead an unbiased mind to the conclusion that Jesus must have visited this country. Regardless of all these certain and sure grounds, no intelligent person can afford to disregard the similarity to be found between the teachings and the ceremonial rites of Buddhism and those of Christianity, especially in Tibet. This resemblance is so close and striking that most Christian researchers believe that Buddhism is the Christianity of the East, and Christianity the Buddhism of the West.[50] Isn't it strange that Jesus said, 'I am the Light and the Way', so said the Buddha. The Gospels call Jesus the Saviour, the Buddha too calls himself the Saviour (see *Lalta Wasatra*). In the Gospels, it is stated that Jesus had no father, and about the Buddha too it is stated that he was born without a father,[51] although apparently, just as Jesus had a foster father Joseph, so had the Buddha a foster father. Similarly, it is stated that a star appeared at the time of the Buddha's birth. Also there is the story of Solomon ordering the cutting of the child in two halves and giving each half to the two women; an exactly similar episode is to be found in the Buddha's *Jataka*.[52] In addition to showing that Jesus did come to this country, it shows that the Jews who had migrated to this land had also established close ties with Buddhism.

The Buddhistic account of the Creation is the same as the one given in the Torah. According to the Torah man is

---

[50] See Appendix, extract 9. (Translator)

[51] See Appendix, extract 3. (Translator)

[52] Stories of the Buddha's former births found in Buddhist literature. (Translator)

considered superior to woman, so is a monk in the religion of the Buddha considered superior to a nun. The Buddha did, however, believe in the transmigration of souls, but his view of transmigration is not opposed to the teaching of the Gospels. According to the Buddha, transmigration is of three kinds:

i. The conduct and courage of a man demands that after death he should be given some kind of a new body.

ii. The kind of transmigration, which the Tibetans believe is peculiar to the Lamas. It means that part of the spirit of some Buddha or Buddha Satwas transmigrates into the Lama for the time being which means that his power, temper and spiritual qualities are transferred into the Lama and begin to animate the recipient.

iii. That in this very life man goes through different creations until on account of his moral qualities he becomes an authentic human being. But before that a time may come when he is, figuratively speaking, a bull; when he grows in greed and evil, he becomes a veritable dog, the first existence giving place to the next, corresponding to the quality of his actions. All these 'metamorphoses', however, take place in this very life. This kind of creed is not opposed to the teaching of the Gospels.

I have already stated that the Buddha also believes in the existence of the Devil; he also believes in heaven and hell, in angels and in the Day of Judgment. The charge that the Buddha did not believe in God, is a pure fabrication. However, he did not believe in Vedanta[53] and in the corporeal gods of the Hindus. He was an acute critic of the

---

[53] The Vedic concept and philosophy of the Divine. (Translator)

Vedas, and did not believe in the truth of the existing Vedas; he believed that they had been corrupted and tampered with. The period during which he was a Hindu and follower of the Vedas, he regarded as the period of evil birth. For example, he hints that for a time he was a monkey, again for a time an elephant, then a deer, a dog, four times a snake, a sparrow, a frog, twice a fish, ten times a tiger, four times a fowl, twice a pig, and once a hare. When he was a hare he used to teach the monkeys, the jackals, and the water dogs. Again, he says that he was once a ghost, once a woman, and once a dancing Devil. All these hints are meant to point to phases of his life as were full of cowardice, effeminacy, impurity, savagery, profligacy, gluttony, and superstition. It appears that in point of fact, his confessions pertain to the time when he was a follower of the Vedas, for, after rejecting them he gives no hint of any evil still clinging to him. On the contrary, he makes great claims. He said that he had become a manifestation of God and had attained *Nirvana*.[54] The Buddha also states that the man who leaves the world accompanied by evil deeds is thrown into hell. Sentinels of hell drag him to the supreme guardian of hell, called Yamah, and the condemned one is asked whether or not he had seen the following Five Messengers who had been sent to warn him:

i. Childhood,

ii. Old age,

iii. Disease,

---

[54] According to Buddhist teaching, Nirvana is the state of perfect bliss attained when the soul is freed from all suffering and absorbed into the supreme spirit. (Translator)

iv. Being punished during one's life as evidence of the punishment in the hereafter,

v. Corpses which remind us of the transitory nature of the world.

The condemned one replies that he had been a fool and that he had not thought over any of these things. The guardians of hell will drag him to the torture chamber and secure him with red-hot iron chains. The Buddha, moreover, says that hell has several zones where sinners of different categories will be cast. In short, all this teaching cries out aloud that the Buddhist religion is to a large extent indebted to the personal example and influence of Jesus. I do not like to elaborate the point further, and should close the section here, because the prophecy about the coming of Jesus to this country has been so clearly spelled out in Buddhist literature; nor can it be denied that the parables and the moral teaching of the Gospels are positively to be found in Buddhist books compiled in Jesus' time. These two points considered together do not leave any doubt about the coming of Jesus to this country. The evidence, therefore, which we wanted to find in Buddhistic records has been discovered in full. God be thanked.

Section Three

Evidence from Historical Writings which Show that Jesus' Journey to the Punjab and Neighbouring Territories was Inevitable

The question naturally arises as to why Jesus, after his escape from the cross, should have come to this country and what could have induced him to take such a long journey? This question requires a little detailed answer and should, therefore, receive a little fuller treatment in the present volume.

Let it be noted, therefore, that it was extremely necessary, by reason of his office as divine messenger, for Jesus to have journeyed to the Punjab and its neighbourhood because the ten tribes of Israel, who in the Gospels have been called the lost sheep of Israel, had migrated to this country. It is a fact which no historian has been able to deny. It was necessary, therefore, that Jesus should have journeyed to this country and, after finding the lost sheep, should have conveyed to them the divine message vouchsafed to him. Had he not done so, the purpose for which he had been sent by God would have remained unfulfilled. His mission was to preach to the lost sheep of Israel. His passing away from the world without seeking the lost sheep, or, after finding them, failing to teach them the way to salvation, would have been quite like the case of a man who had been charged by his king to go to a desert tribe to dig a well and supply them with water, but who goes instead to some other place where he spends three or four years, taking no steps to search for the concerned tribe. Does such a man carry out the command of the king? Not in the least. The man cares not for that tribe, he merely looks to his own comfort.

If, however, it is asked, how and why it should be supposed that the ten tribes of Israel had come to this country, the answer is that the supporting evidence of this thesis is so strong and incontrovertible that even a dullard will not deny it. It is too well known that people like the Afghans and the old inhabitants of Kashmir are in fact of

Israelite origin. For example, the people of Alai Kohistan which is at a distance of two or three days' journey from the district of Hazara, have called themselves Beni Israel from time immemorial. Similarly, there is another hilly tract in this region known as Kala Dakah, whose inhabitants also take pride in being of Israelite origin. Then in the Hazara district itself, there is a tribe which claims to belong to the house of Israel. Similarly, the inhabitants of the mountain range between Chillas and Kabul also call themselves Israelites. Dr. Bernier's view about the people of Kashmir, which is based on the authority of some English scholars, and is expressed in the second part of his book *Travels,* is only too true. According to him, the Kashmiri people are the descendants of Israel; their dress, their features and some of their rituals conclusively point to the fact that they are undoubtedly of Israelite origin.[55] An Englishman, Forster by name, writes in his book that during his stay in Kashmir he felt as if he was living amidst a tribe of the Jews.[56] H. W. Bellews C.S.I. in his book *The Races of Afghanistan,* published by Thacker Spink & Co. Calcutta, states that the Afghans came from Syria. Nebuchadnezzar took them prisoner and settled them in Persia and Media, from whence at a later date they moved to the East and settled in the Ghor hills, where they were known as Beni Israel. In proof of this there is the prophecy of the Prophet Idris (Enoch), which says that the ten tribes of Israel who were taken prisoner, escaped from captivity and took refuge in the territory called Arsarah which appears to be another name of the area

---

[55] See Appendix, extract 10. (Translator)
[56] See Appendix, extract 11. (Translator)

known as Hazara today, part of the region being called Ghor. In *Tabaqaat-i-Naasri,* there is an account of the conquest of Afghanistan by Genghis Khan. It is stated that in the times of the Shabnisi dynasty there lived a tribe known as Beni Israel, some of whom were big businessmen and good traders. In 622 A.D., which is the year of the Holy Prophet Muhammad's[sa] Call, these people were to be found in the eastern part of Herat. A Quraish chief Khalid bin Walid brought to them the tidings of the Prophet's Coming with a view to bringing them under the banner of the Divine Messenger[sa]. Five or six chiefs were elected to accompany him, of whom the principal chief was Qais, whose other name was Kish. After accepting Islam, these people fought bravely for the cause of Islam and made many conquests. The Holy Prophet[sa] gave them many presents on their return journey, blessed them, and prophesied that they would attain great power and ascendancy. The Holy Prophet[sa] also prophesied that the chiefs of this tribe would always be known as Maliks. He gave Qais the name of Abdul Rashid and conferred upon him the title *Pahtaan.* Afghan writers say that this is a Syriac word which means a rudder. As the newly converted Qais was, like the rudder of a ship, a guide to his tribe, he was awarded the title *Pahtaan.*

It is not known at what point of time the Afghans of Ghor advanced farther and came to settle in the territory around Kandhar, which is their home today. This happened probably in the first century of the Islamic calendar. The Afghans maintain that Qais married the daughter of Khalid bin Walid, by whom he had three sons whose names were Saraban, Patan, and Gurgasht. Saraban had two sons, called

Sacharj Yun, and Karsh Yun. It is their descendants who are today known as the Afghans or Beni-Israel. The people of Asia-Minor, and Muslim historians of the West, call Afghans *Sulaimanis*.[57]

In *The Cyclopaedia of India, Eastern and Southern Asia*, by Edward Balfour, Vol. III,[58] it is stated that the Jewish people are spread all over the central, southern, and eastern regions of Asia. In early times these people were settled in large numbers in China; they had a synagogue at Yih Chu, the headquarter of the district of Shu. Dr. Wolf, who wandered for a long time in search of the ten lost tribes of Beni Israel, is of the opinion that if Afghans are the progeny of Jacob, they belong to the tribes of Yahuda and Bin Yamin. Another report proves that the Jews were exiled to Tartary; they were found in large numbers in the territories round about Bukhara, Merv and Khiva. Prester John, Emperor of Tartary, in his letter to Alexis Comminus, the Emperor of Constantinople, writing about his dominions, says that beyond the river Amu there are the ten tribes of Israel who, though they claim to be under their own king, are in reality his subjects and vassals. Dr. Moore's researches show that the Tartar tribe named Chosan is of Jewish origin and that among them are to be found traces of the ancient Jewish faith. For example, they still practise the rite of circumcision. The Afghans have a tradition that they are the ten lost tribes of Israel. After the sack of Jerusalem, the king Nebuchadnezzar took them prisoner and settled them in Ghor, near Bamiyan. Before the arrival of Khalid bin Walid

---

[57] See Appendix, extract 12. (Translator)
[58] It should be volume I, third edition. (Translator)

they had consistently held fast to the Jewish faith.

In appearance, the Afghans resemble the Jews in all respects. Like them, the younger brother marries the widow of the elder brother. A French traveller, Ferrier by name, who passed through Herat, states that Israelites are found in large numbers in that territory, and that they have full liberty in the practice of their religion.[59] The Rabbi Bin Yamin of Toledo, Spain in the twelfth century A.D. ventured out in search of the lost tribes. He states that these Jews are settled in China, Iran and Tibet. Josephus, who wrote the ancient history of the Jews in 93 A.D., in the course of his account of the Jews who escaped from bondage along with the Prophet Ezra, states in his eleventh book that the ten tribes were settled beyond the Euphrates even at that time, and that their numbers were uncountable.[60] By 'beyond the Euphrates' he meant Persia and the eastern territories. St. Jerome who lived in the fifth century A.D., writing about Prophet Hosea says in the margin, in support of his thesis, that since that day the ten tribes (of the Israelites) have been under king Parthya or Paras, and have not been released from bondage. In the first volume of the same book, it is stated that Count Juan Steram testifies on page 233-34 of his book that the Afghans admit that Nebuchadnezzar, after the destruction of the Temple at Jerusalem, exiled them to the territory of Bamiyan (which is adjacent to Ghor, in Afghanistan).

On page 166 of the book, *A Narrative of a Visit to Ghuzni, Kabul and Afghanistan* by G. T. Vigne, F.G.S. (1840), it is

---

[59] See Appendix, extract 13,14,15. (Translator)
[60] See Appendix, extract 16. (Translator)

stated that one Mullah Khuda Dad quoted in his presence from a book called *Majma-ul-Ansaab*, that the eldest son of Jacob was Judas, whose son was Usrak; Usrak's son was Aknur; Aknur's son was Maalib; Maalib's Farlai; Farlai's Qais, Qais' Talut; Talut's Armea, and Armea's son was Afghan whose descendants are the Afghan people and after whom the latter are named. Afghan, a contemporary of Nebuchadnezzar, was known as a descendant of Israel, and had forty sons. In the 34th generation of his genealogical tree, after some 2000 years, was born Qais who lived in the time of the Holy Prophet Muhammad[sa]. His descendants multiplied down to 64 generations.[61] Afghan's eldest son, Salm, migrated from his Syrian home and settled in Ghor Mashkoh, near Herat, and his descendants spread into Afghanistan.[62]

In *A cyclopedia of Geography* by James Bryce, F.G.S. (London, 1856), on page 11, it is stated that the Afghans trace their genealogy to Saul, the Israelite King, and call themselves the descendants of Israel. Alexander Burns says that the Afghans state that they are of Jewish origin; that the King of Babel captured them and settled them in the territory of Ghor which lies to the northwest of Kabul; that up to 622 A.D. they continued to hold on to the Jewish faith, but that Khalid bin Abdullah (Abdullah has been written mistakenly instead of Walid) married the daughter of a chief of this tribe and made them accept Islam in that year.[63]

On page 39 of Col. G. B. Malleson's book *History of*

---

[61] It should be read as 66. (Translator)
[62] See Appendix, extract 17. (Translator)
[63] See Appendix, extract 18. (Translator)

Afghanistan (London 1878), it is stated that Abdullah Khan of Herat, the French traveller named Ferrier, and Sir William Jones, a recognised orientalist, agree that the Afghan people are descended from the Beni-Israel, and that they are the descendants of the ten lost tribes.[64] The book *History of the Afghans*, by G. P. Ferrier,[65] translated by Capt. William Jesse, and published in London (1858), records on page 1 that the majority of oriental historians are of the opinion that the Afghan people are the descendants of the ten tribes of Israel and that the Afghans too hold the same opinion. The same historian says on page 4 of this book, that Afghans possess evidence that at Peshawar, during his invasion of India, Nadir Shah was presented by the chiefs of the Yoosoofzyes tribe with a Bible written in Hebrew as well as several other articles preserved by their families for the performance of religious rites of their old faith. There were also Jews in Nadir Shah's camp, who, on seeing the articles, readily recognised them. Again, the same historian states on page 4 of his book that in his opinion Abdullah Khan's view is highly reliable. Briefly stated this view is as follows: Malek Thalut (Saul) had two sons, Afghan and Djalut. Afghan was the patriarch of these people. After the reigns of David and Solomon, the Israelite tribes started fighting one another. As a result, each tribe became separated from the other. This state of affairs continued up to the time of Nebuchadnezzar who invaded and killed 70,000 Jews. He sacked the city, and took the remaining

---

[64] See Appendix, extract 19. (Translator)
[65] This should be J.P. Ferrier (Joseph Pierre Ferrier). In Urdu *J* (ﺝ) was written as *G* (ﺝ) because, at the time of the author, not much distinction was made between ﺝ and ﺡ. (Translator)

Jews with him to Babel as prisoners. After this catastrophe, the children of Afghan fled in fear from Judea to Arabia and remained there for a long time. But as water and land were scarce, and man and beast suffered great hardship, they decided to migrate to India. A party of Abdalees remained in Arabia, and during the Khilafat of Hadhrat Abu Bakr one of their chiefs established matrimonial relationship with Khalid bin Walid.... When Iran fell to Arabia, these people migrated from Arabia and settled in the Iranian provinces of Fars and Kirman. They stayed there till Genghis Khan's invasion. As the Abdalees were helpless against the atrocities of Genghis Khan, they left for India via Makran, Sindh and Multan. But here too they couldn't find peace. They eventually arrived at Koh Sulaiman and settled there. The other members of the Abdali tribe also joined them. They consisted of 24 tribes, all descendants of Afghan who had three sons, Tsera-Bend (Saraban), Arkash (Argoutch) and Karlen (Batan). They had eight sons each who multiplied into twenty-four tribes, each tribe was named after each son. The names of the sons and the tribes are given below:[66]

Sons of Tsera-Bend	Name of tribe
Abdal	Abdalees
Yoosoof	Yoosoofzyes
Baboor	Baboorees
Wezir	Wezirees
Lohooan	Lohooanees

---

[66] See Appendix, extract 20. (Translator)

Beritch	Beritchees
Khooguian	Khooguianees
Chiran	Chiranees

Sons of Gargasht (Arkash)	
Ghildj	Ghildjzyes
Kauker	Kaukerees
Djumourian	Djumourianees
Storian	Storianees
Pen	Penees
Kass	Kassees
Takan	Takanees
Nassar	Nassarees

Sons of Kerlen	
Khattak	Khattakees
Soor	Soorees
Afreed	Afreedees
Toor	Toorees
Zaz	Zazees
Bab	Babees
Benguech	Benguechees
Lendeh-poor	Lendeh-poorees

The book, Makhzan-i-Afghani[*] by Khawaja Nimatullah

---

[*] See page 3 of preface by the author. This book is a summary of authentic chronicles like Tarikh-e-Tibri, Majma-ul-Ansaab, Gazida Jahankushai, Matla-ul-Anwaar and Maadan-e-Akbar. (Author)

of Herat, was written in 1018 Hijra during the reign of the Emperor Jahangir, and was translated and published by Prof. Bernhard Doran of Kharkov University in 1836 in London. It contains the following statements in the chapters mentioned below:

In chapter 1 there is the history of Jacob Israel with whom starts the genealogy of the Afghans.

In chapter II there is the history of King Talut, the genealogy of the Afghans is traced to Talut. On pages 22 and 23 it is stated: Talut had two sons, Berkhia and Ermiah. Berkhia had a son, Asif and Ermiah's Afghan and on page 24 it is stated that Afghan had twenty-four[67] sons and no one among the Israelites could compare in numbers with the descendants of Afghan. On page 65[68] it is stated that Bokhtnasser[69] occupied the whole of *Sham* (Syria), etc., exiled the Israelite tribes and forced them to settle in the mountainous regions of Ghor, Ghazneen, Kabul, Candahar and Koh Firoz, where the descendants of Asif and Afghan particularly took up their abode.

The third chapter contains the statement that when Bokhtnasser expelled the Israelites from Syria, some tribes who were the descendants of Asif and Afghan took refuge in Arabia. The Arabs used to address them as Beni Israel and Beni Afghan.[70]

On pages 37 and 38 of the same book, on the authority of

---

[67] It should be read as 'forty', as is stated in extract 21 of the Appendix. (Translator)

[68] This is a misprint, to be read as page 25. See Appendix, extract 21. (Translator)

[69] Nebuchadnezzar (Translator)

[70] Meaning the children of Israel and the children of Afghan. (Translator)

the author of *Majma'ul Ansaab*, and that of Mestoufi, the author of *Taareekh Gozeeda*, it is stated that in the lifetime of the Holy Prophet[sa], Khalid bin Walid invited the Afghans to Islam, who, after Bokhtnasser's invasion, had taken up residence in the Ghor territory. The Afghan chiefs under the leadership of Qais, who was Talut's descendant in the 37th generation, came to pay their homage to the Holy Prophet[sa]. Qais was named Abdul Rashid by the Holy Prophet[sa] (Here the genealogy of Abdul Rashid Qais is traced back to Talut—Saul). The Holy Prophet[sa] also conferred the title of Pathan on the chiefs which means 'ship's rudder'. After some time the chiefs returned to their territory and began to preach Islam.

In the same book *Makhzan-i-Afghani* on page 63, it is recorded that Farid-ud-Din Ahmad makes the following statement concerning the titles Beni Afghanah or Beni Afghan, in his book *Risalah Ansaab-i-Afghaniyyah*: After Nebuchadnezzar, the Magian, had subjugated the Israelites, conquered the Syrian territories and sacked Jerusalem, he took the Israelites prisoners and exiled them as slaves. He took away with him several of their tribes who followed the Mosaic Law, and ordered them to renounce their ancestral faith and to worship him instead of God, which they refused to do. Consequently, Nebuchadnezzar put to death two thousand of the most intelligent and the wisest from among them and ordered the rest to leave his kingdom and Syria. Some of them left Nebuchadnezzar's territory under a chief and went away to the Ghor hills. Their descendants settled down in that place, multiplied at a fast rate, and people began to designate them as Beni Israel, Beni Asif and Beni Afghan.

On page 64, the same author says that reliable records like *Taarikh-i-Afghani, Taarikh-i-Ghori,* etc., contain the assertion that the Afghans are mostly Beni Israel and some of them are of Coptic origin. Moreover, Abul Fazl also states that some Afghans regard themselves as of Egyptian origin, the reason given by them being that when the Beni Israel returned to Egypt from Jerusalem, this tribe, namely, the Afghans migrated to India. On page 64 Farid-ud-Din Ahmad writes about the title 'Afghan' that some writers are on record having said that after exile (from Syria) they used always to 'bewail and cry' in remembrance of their home. That is why they were named Afghans.[71] Sir John Malcolm is also of the same opinion; vide *History of Persia,* Vol. I, page 101.

On page 63, is given Mahabat Khan's statement that: 'As they are the followers and relations of Solomon, they are, therefore, styled Sulaimanis by the Arabs'.

On page 65, it is written that investigations of almost all oriental historians show that the Afghan people's own view is that they are of Jewish origin. Some of the present day historians have adopted the same view and regard it as true or very nearly true....

The translator Bernard Dorn's contention that the adoption of Jewish names by Afghans is due to their having accepted Islam is not sustained by evidence. In north western and western Punjab, there are tribes of Hindu origin who have become Muslims but whose names are not after the names of the Jewish people, which clearly shows

---

[71] Meaning that the title 'Afghan' is a combination of two Persian words 'Aah' (lament) and 'Faghan' (cry of pain). (Translator)

that by becoming Muslim people do not necessarily adopt Jewish names.

That in features the Afghans have a surprising resemblance to the Jews, is a fact which is admitted even by such scholars as do not at all subscribe to the Afghan claim that they are of Jewish origin. This is the only proof strong enough to establish that the Afghan are of Jewish origin. Sir John Malcolm's remarks in this connection are as follows: "Although the Afghans' right to this proud (Jewish) descent is very doubtful, it is evident from their personal appearance and many of their customs that they (the Afghans) are a distinct race from the Persians, Tartars and Indians and this alone seems to give some credibility to the Afghan claim which is otherwise contradicted by many strong facts, and of which no direct proof has been produced. If similarity of features between one people and another can point to anything, the Kashmiris with their Jewish features would certainly be found to be of Jewish origin. This has been mentioned not only by Bernier but also by Forster, and possibly by other scholars." Although Forster does not accept Bernier's opinion, he concedes that when he was among the Kashmiris he thought he was living amidst a Jewish people.[72]

Under the word 'Cashmere', on page 250 of A. K. Johnston's Dictionary of Geography, there is this statement:

The natives are of a tall, robust frame of body, with manly features, the women full-formed and handsome, with an acquiline nose and features, resembling the Jewish.[73]

---

[72] See Appendix, extract 21. (Translator)
[73] See Appendix, extract 22. (Translator)

The *Civil & Military Gazette* of 23 November 1898 on page
4 under the heading *Sawati and Afridi,* reproduces a very
valuable   and   interesting   paper   presented   to   the
Anthropological section of the British Association at one of
its recent meetings, which will be read at its winter session
before the Committee on Anthropological Research. The
Gazette says:

> *The original Pathan or Paktan inhabitants of these western
> gates of India are recognised in very early history, many of
> the tribes being mentioned by Herodotus and the historians
> of Alexander. In mediaeval times the rough uncultivated
> wilderness of mountains they held was called Roh, and its
> inhabitants Rohillas, and there can be little doubt that most
> of these early Rohilla or Pathan tribes were in their places
> long before the overlying Afghan tribes were thought of. All
> Afghans whatsoever now counted as Pathans, because they
> all speak the Pathan language, Pushto, they acknowledge no
> direct kinship, claiming themselves to be Beni Israel, the
> descendants of those tribes who were carried captive to
> Babylon by Nebuchadnezzar. All of them have, however,
> adopted the Pushto tongue, and all recognise the same
> Pathan   code   of   common   civil   observances   called
> Paktanwali, which is, in many of its provisions, curiously
> suggestive both of the old Mosaic dispensation and of
> ancient observances of the Rajput races.*

> *Thus the Pathans, with whom we have lately been so largely
> concerned, may be divided into two great communities, i.e.
> tribes and clans such as Waziris, Afridis, Orakzais, etc. who
> are of Indian origin, and those who are Afghans, who claim
> to be Semitic and who represent the dominant race
> throughout our frontier; and it seems at least to be possible
> that the Paktanwali, which is an unwritten code and which
> is acknowledged by them all alike, may be of very mixed
> origin indeed. We may find in it Mosaic ordinances grafted
> on to Rajput traditions and modified by Moslem custom. The
> Afghans, who call themselves Duranis and who have done so*

ever since the foundation of the Durani Empire about a century and a half ago, say that they trace their descent from the Israelitish tribes through an ancestor named Kish (Qais), to whom the prophet Mohomet gave the name Pathan (which is Syriac for a rudder), because he was to steer his people into the currents of Islam.... It is difficult to account for the universal prevalence of Israelitish names amongst Afghans without admitting some early connection with the Israelitish nation. Still more difficult is it to account for certain observances, such for instance as the keeping of the Feast of the Passover (which, by the Yusufzai branch of the Afghan race, is at most curiously well imitated) or for the persistence with which the least educated Afghans maintain this tradition, without some original basis of truth for it. Bellew thinks that this Israelitish connection may be a real one, but he points out that one at least of the three main branches of the Afghan family traditionally sprung from Kish (Qais), is called by the name Sarabaur, which is but the Pushto form of the ancient name applied to the solar race of Rajputs, colonies of whom are known to have immigrated into Afghanistan after their defeat by the Chandrabans, the lunar race in the great contest, the Mahabharat of early Indian records. Thus the Afghan may possibly be an Israelite absorbed into ancient Rajput tribes, and this has always appeared to me to be the most probable solution of the problem of his origin. Anyhow, the modern Afghan takes his stand, on the grounds of tradition, to be one of the chosen race, a descendant of Abraham....

We have reproduced all these quotations from the writings of well-known authors, and if considered together, they will convince the impartial reader that Afghans and Kashmiris, who are to be found in India, on the frontier and in its neighbourhood, are really the Beni Israel. In the second part of this book, God willing, I shall prove in greater detail that the ultimate object underlying Jesus' long journey to India was that he might discharge the duty of preaching to all the Israelite tribes, a fact to which he has alluded in the Gospels. It is not surprising, therefore, that he should have come to India and Kashmir. On the contrary, it would indeed be surprising if, without discharging his duties as prophet, he should have ascended to the heavens and taken his seat there. With this, we close this part of the discussion.

Peace be on those who are guided aright.

MIRZA GHULAM AHMAD,
The Promised Messiah,
Qadian, District Gurdaspur.

Appendix

Extracts from the Original Books which have been
Quoted by the Author in 'Jesus in India'.

1

Lectures on the Origin and Growth of Religion as
Illustrated by some Points in the History of **Indian
Buddhism**, by T. W. Rhys Davids, (the Hibbert Lectures ,
1881) (Williams & Norgate, London 1881)

Page 147. 'All this is of peculiar interest from the comparative point
of view. It is an expression from the Buddhist standpoint, which
excludes the theory of a Supreme Deity, of an idea very similar to
that which is expressed in Christian writings when Christ is
represented as the manifestation of God to men, the Logos, the Word
of God made flesh, the Bread of Life. And it is not a mere chance that
heterodox followers of the two religions have afterwards used the
Buddha and the Logos conceptions as bases of their emanation
theories. It is only a fresh instance of the way in which similar ideas
in similarly constituted minds come to be modified in very similar
ways. The Cakka-vatti Buddha was to the early Buddhists what the
Messiah Logos was to the early Christians. In both cases the two
ideas overlap one another, run into one another, supplement one
another. In both cases, the two combined cover as nearly the same
ground as the different foundations of the two teachings will permit.
And it is the Cakka-vatti Buddha circle of ideas in the one case, just
as the Messiah Logos in the other, that has had the principal
influence in determining the opinions of the early disciples as to the
person of their Master. The method followed in the early Buddhist
and early Christian biographies of their respective Masters was the
same, and led to similar results; though the details are in no
particular quite identical in the two cases.'

2

Buddhism, in its Connexion with Brāhmanism and Hindūism, and in its Contrast with Christianity, by Sir Monier Monier-Williams, K.C.I.E., Second Edition, (John Murray, London 1890)

Pages 134-135. 'He said of himself (Mahā-vagga 1.6,8), — 'I am the all- subduer (sabbābhibhū); the all- wise; I have no stains; through myself I possess knowledge; I have no rival (patipuggalo); I am the chief Arhat— the highest teacher; I alone am the absolutely wise (Sambuddha); I am the Conqueror (Jina); all the fires of desire are quenched (sītibhūto) in me; I have Nirvāna (nibbuto).'

Page 135 *(foot- note)*. 'In fact Gautama remained a Bodhi-sattva until he was thirty-four or thirty-five, when he attained perfect enlightenment and Buddhahood.'

Page 126. '1. Kill not any living thing. 2. Steal not. 3. Commit not adultery. 4. Lie not. 5. Drink not strong drink....
6. Eat no food except at stated times. 7. Use no wreaths, ornaments, or perfumes. 8. Use no high or broad bed, but only a mat on the ground. 9. Abstain from dancing, singing, music, and worldly spectacles. 10. Own no gold, or silver of any kind, and accept none. (Mahā-vagga 1.56). [This Buddhist Dasa-sīla may be contrasted with the Mosaic Decalogue.]'

Pages 45-47. 'The Buddha's early disciples were not poor men; for the sixth to be admitted to the Sangha was a high-born youth named Yasa.....
In sending forth these sixty monks to proclaim his own gospel of deliverance, he addressed them thus:-
'I am delivered from all fetters (p.127), human and divine. You too, O monks, are freed from the same fetters. Go forth and wander everywhere, out of compassion for the world and for the welfare of gods and men. Go forth, one by one, in different directions. Preach the doctrine (Dharmam), salutary (kalyāna) in its beginning, middle, and end, in its spirit (artha) and in its letter (vyañjana). Proclaim a life of perfect restraint, chastity, and celibacy (brahmaćariyam). I will

go also to preach this doctrine' (Mahā-vagga I. II. I).

When his monk-missionaries had departed, Gautama himself followed, though not till Māra (p. 41) had again tempted him. Quitting Benares he journeyed back to Uruvelā, near Gayā. There he first converted thirty rich young men and then one thousand orthodox Brāhmans, led by Kāsyapa and his two brothers, who maintained a sacred fire ('Brāhmanism,' p. 364). The fire-chamber was haunted by a fiery snake-demon; so Buddha asked to accupy the room for a night, fought the serpent and confined him in his own alms-bowl. Next he worked other miracles (said to have been 3500 in number)....

To them on a hill Gayāsīsa (Brahma-yoni), near Gayā, he preached his 'burning' fire-sermon (Mahā-vº I. 21): 'Everything, O monks, is burning (ādittam=ādīptam). The eye is burning; visible things are burning. The sensation produced by contact with visible things is burning—burning with fire of lust (desire), enmity and delusion (rāgagginā dosagginā mohagginā), with birth, decay (jarayā), death, grief, lamentation, pain, dejection (domanassehi), and despair (upāyāsehi). The ear is burning; sounds are burning; the nośe is burning, odours are burning; the tongue is burning, tastes are burning; the body is burning, objects of sense are burning. The mind is burning; thoughts are burning. All are burning with the fire of passions and lusts. Observing this, O monks, a wise and noble disciple becomes weary of (or disgusted with) the eye, weary of visible things, weary of the ear, weary of sounds, weary of odours, weary of tastes, weary of the body, weary of the mind. Becoming weary, he frees himself from passions and lusts. When free, he realizes that his object is accomplished, that he has lived a life of restraint and chastity (brahmaćariyam), that re-birth is ended.'

It is said that this fire-sermon—which is a key to the meaning of Nirvāna—was suggested by the sight of a conflagration. It was Gautama's custom to impress ideas on his hearers by pointing to visible objects. He compares all life to a flame; and the gist of the discourse is the duty of extinguishing the fire of lusts, and with it the fire of all existence, and importance of monkhood and celibacy for the attainment of this end.

Contrast in Christ's Sermon on the Mount the words addressed to

the multitude (not to monks), 'Blessed are the pure in heart, for they shall see God.'
The Buddha and his followers next proceeded to Rājagriha.'

3

Buddhism: being a Sketch of the Life and Teachings of Gautama, the Buddha, by T. W. Rhys Davids, M.A. Ph.D. (Society for Promoting Christian Knowledge, London 1882)

Page 183. 'His mother was the best and the purest of the daughters of men.'

In the footnote of page 183, Davids quotes St. Jerome:

'St. Jerome says (contra Jovian. bk. I): 'It is handed down as a tradition among the Gymnosophists of India, that Buddha, the founder of their system, was brought forth by a virgin from her side.'

4

The **Life of the Buddha** and the Early History of his Order, derived from Tibetan Works in the Bkah-Hgyur and Bstan-Hgyur, translated by W. Woodville Rockhill (Trübner & Co. London 1884)

Page 32. 'The rumour had reached Kapilavastu that the prince had died under the excess of his penances, and all the court was plunged in despair, and his wives fell fainting to the ground; but a little after came the news that he had attained enlightenment, and great was the rejoicing everywhere.'

Page 141. 'As soon as the Blessed One expired the mighty earth was shaken, thunderbolts did fall, and the gods in the sky did shriek with (or like) sound of drum (f.635ᵃ). At that time the venerable Mahâkâçyapa was stopping in the Kalantakanivasa Bamboo grove at Râjagriha; and when the earth quaked he sought what might be the reason, and he saw that the Blessed One had utterly passed away...'

5

Buddha: His Life, His Doctrine, His Order by Dr. Hermann Oldenberg, Translated from the German by William Hoey, M.A., D.Lit. (Williams & Norgate, London 1882)

Page 142 *(foot-note):* 'On the occasion of a prophecy of Buddha's regarding Metteyya, the next Buddha, who will in the far future appear upon the earth, it is said: "He will be the leader of a band of disciples, numbering hundreds of thousands, as I am now the leader of bands of disciples, numbering hundreds." — *Cakkavattisuttanta.'*

Page 419. 'Regarding the wife and child of Buddha the chief passage is "Mahâvagga," i, 54; Râhula is frequently mentioned in the Sutta texts as Buddha's son, without any prominent *rôle* being ascribed to him among the circles of disciples by the ancient tradition.'

Page 103. 'He *(Buddha)* says: "Râhula is born to me, a fetter has been forged for me."'

Page 103 *(foot-note).* 'In the name Râhula there seems to be an allusion to Râhu, the sun and moon subduing (darkening) demon.'

6

Tibet, Tartary and Mongolia; their Social and Political Condition, and the Religion of Boodh, as there Existing, by Henry T. Prinsep Esq. Second Edition (Wm. H. Allen & Co. London 1852)

Pages 12-14. 'The earliest travels into Tibet Proper which have been transmitted to us, are those of the Jesuit fathers, Grueber and Dorville, who returned from China by that route in A.D. 1661, just four hundred years after Marco Polo's journey westward. They were the first Christians of Europe who are known to have penetrated into the populous parts of Tibet; for Marco Polo's journey was, as we have stated, to the north-west, by the sources of the Oxus. Father Grueber was much struck with the extraordinary similitude he found, as well in the doctrine, as in the rituals, of the Boodhists of Lassa to those of his own Romish faith. He noticed first, that the dress of Lamas corresponded with that handed down to us in ancient paintings, as the dress of the Apostles. 2nd. That the discipline of the monasteries, and of the different orders of Lamas or priests, bore the same resemblance to that of the Romish church. 3rd. That the notion of an incarnation was common to both, so also the belief in paradise and purgatory. 4th. He remarked that they made suffrages, alms, prayers, and sacrifices for the dead, like the Roman Catholics. 5th. That they had convents, filled with monks and friars, to the number of 30,000, near Lassa, who all made the three vows of poverty, obedience, and chastity, like Roman monks, besides other vows. And 6th, that they had confessors, licensed by the superior Lamas, or bishops; and so empowered to receive confessions, and to impose penances, and give absolution. Besides all this, there was found the practice of using holy water, of singing service in alternation, of praying for the dead, and a perfect similarity in the costumes of the great and superior Lamas to those of the different orders of the Romish hierarchy. These early missionaries, further, were led to conclude, from what they saw and heard, that the ancient books of the Lamas contained traces of the Christian religion, which must, they thought, have been preached in Tibet in the time of the Apostles.'

Then concerning the advent of a Saviour, the author H. T. Prinsep writes in the same book (Tibet, Tartary and Mongolia) on page 171:

'The general expectation of the birth of a great prophet, Redeemer, or Saviour, which is alluded to even by Tacitus, as prevailing at the period when the founder of the Christian religion appeared, was, there can be no doubt, of Boodhistic origin, and not at all confined to Jews, or based only on the prophecies of their Scripture.'

As a foot-note on page 171 the author further wrote:
'The advent of another Boodh a thousand years after Gotama, or Sakhya Muni, is distinctly prophesied in the Pitakattayan and Atthakatha. Gotama declares himself to be the twenty-fifth Boodh, and says, "Bagawa Metteyo is yet to come." The name Metteyo bears an extraordinary resemblance to Messiah.'

7

A Record of **The Buddhist Religion** as Practised in India and the Malay Archipelago (A.D. 671-695) by I-Tsing, Translated by J. Takakusu, B.A., Ph.D. (Oxford, Clarendon Press 1896)

pages 223-224: 'It is indeed curious to find the name of MESSIAH in a Buddhist work, though the name comes in quite accidentally. The book is called 'The New Catalogue of the Buddhist Books compiled in the Chêng Yüan Period' (A.D. 785-804), in the new Japanese edition of the Chinese Buddhist Books (Bodleian Library, Jap. 65 DD, 結六, P. 73; this book is not in Nanjio's Catalogue)....

Moreover, the Sanghârâma of the Sâkya and the monastery of Tâ-ch'in (Syria) differ much in their customs, and their religious practices are entirely opposed to each other. King-ching (Adam) ought to hand down the teaching of MESSIAH (Mi-shi-ho), and the Sâkyaputriya-Sramaṇas should propagate the Sûtras of the Buddha.'

8

The **Nineteenth Century**: a Monthly Review, edited by James Knowles, Vol. XXXVI, July-December 1894 (Sampson Low, Marston & Co. London 1894)

Page 517. 'But M. Notovitch, though he did not bring the manuscripts home, at all events saw them, and not pretending to a knowledge of Tibetan, had the Tibetan text translated by an interpreter, and has published seventy pages of it in French in his *Vie inconnue de Jésus-Christ.* He was evidently prepared for the discovery of a Life of Christ among the Buddhists. Similarities between Christianity and Buddhism have frequently been pointed out of late, and the idea that Christ was influenced by Buddhist doctrines has more than once been put forward by popular writers. The difficulty has hitherto been to discover any real historical channel through which Buddhism could have reached Palestine at the time of Christ. M. Notovitch thinks that the manuscript which he found at Himis explains the matter in the simplest way. There is no doubt, as he says, a gap in the life of Christ, say from his fifteenth to his twenty-ninth year. During that very time the new Life found in Tibet asserts that Christ was in India, that he studied Sanskrit and Pâli, that he read the Vedas and the Buddhist Canon, and then returned through Persia to Palestine to preach the Gospel. If we understand M. Notovitch rightly, this Life of Christ was taken down from the mouths of some Jewish merchants who came to India immediately after the Crucifixion (P. 237). It was written down in Pâli, the sacred language of Southern Buddhism; the scrolls were afterwards brought from India to Nepaul and Makhada (*quære* Magadha) about 200 A.D. (P. 236), and from Nepaul to Tibet, and are at present carefully preserved at Lassa. Tibetan translations of the Pâli text are found, he says, in various Buddhist monasteries, and, among the rest, at Himis. It is these Tibetan manuscripts which were translated at Himis for M. Notovitch while he was laid up in the monastery with a broken leg, and it is from these manuscripts that he has taken his new Life of Jesus Christ and published it in French, with an account of his travels. This volume, which has already passed through several editions in France, is soon to be translated into English.'

9

The **Mystery of the Ages** contained in the Secret Doctrine of all Religions. By Marie, Countess of Caithness, Duchesse De Pomár (C. L. H. Wallace, Philanthropic Reform Publisher, Oxford Mansion, W.

London 1887)

On Page 145 *the author says about 'Buddhism':* ..... It is the Christianity of the East, and, as such, even in better conservation than is Christianity, the Buddhism of the West.'

10

Travels in the **Mogul Empire** A.D. 1656-1668 by François Bernier, Translated, on the basis of Irving Brock's version and annotated by Archibald Constable 1891, Second Edition, revised by Vincent A. Smith, M.A. (Oxford University Press 1916)

Page 430. 'There are, however, many signs of *Judaism* to be found in this country. On entering the Kingdom after crossing the *Pire-penjale* mountains, the inhabitants in the frontier villages struck me as resembling *Jews*. Their countenance and manner, and that indescribable peculiarity which enables a traveller to distinguish the inhabitants of different nations, all seemed to belong to that ancient people. You are not to ascribe what I say to mere fancy, the *Jewish* appearance of these villagers having been remarked by our *Jesuit Father,* and by several other *Europeans,* long before I visited *Kachemire.'*

11

A **Journey from Bengal to England**, through the Northern Part of India, Kashmire, Afghanistan, and Perisa, and into Russia by the Caspian-Sea, by George Forster, vol. II (R. Faulder and Son, London 1808)

Page 23. 'On first seeing these people in their own country, I imagined, from their garb, the cast of countenance, which is long, and of a grave aspect, and the form of their beards, that I had come amongst a nation of Jews.'

12

The **Races of Afghanistan**, being a Brief Account of the Principal Nations Inhabiting that Country, by Surgeon-Major H. W. Bellew, C.S.I. (Thacker, Spink & Co. Calcutta, (1880) MDCCCLXXX)

Page15. 'The traditions of this people refer them to Syria as the country of their residence at the time they were carried away into captivity by Bukhtunasar (Nebuchadnezzar), and planted as colonists in different parts of Persia and Media. From these positions they, at some subsequent period, emigrated eastward into the mountainous country of Ghor, where they were called by the neighbouring peoples "Bani Afghan" and "Bani Israíl," or children of Afghan, and children of Israel. In corroboration of this we have the testimony of the prophet Esdras to the effect that the ten tribes of Israel, who were carried into captivity, subsequently escaped and found refuge in the country of Arsareth, which is supposed to be identical with the Hazarah country of the present day, and of which Ghor forms a part. It is also stated in the Tabacati Nasiri—a historical work which contains, among other information, a detailed account of the conquest of this country by Changhiz Khan— that in the time of the native Shansabi dynasty there was a people called Bani Israíl living in that country, and that some of them were extensively engaged in trade with the countries around.

This people was settled in the Ghor country, to the east of Herat, at the time that Muhammad announced his mission as the Prophet of God— about 622 A.D. And it was there that Khalid-bin-Walíd, a chief of the Curesh tribe of Arabs, came to them with the tidings of the new faith, and an invitation to join the Prophet's standard.'

Page 16. '...... the mission of Khalid was not without success, for he returned to the Prophet, accompanied by a deputation of six or seven representative men of the Afghan people and their followers amounting in all to seventy-six persons. The chief or leader of this party was named Kais or Kish.

The traditions of the people go on to the effect that this Kais and his companions fought so well and successfully in the cause of the Prophet, that Muhammad, on dismissing them to their homes, presented them with handsome gifts, complimented them on their bravery, and giving them his blessing foretold a glorious career for their nation, and promised that the title of Malik (or king) should distinguish their chiefs for ever.... At the same time the Prophet, as a mark of special favour and distinction, was pleased to change the Hebrew name of Kais to the Arab one of Abdur Rashíd— "the servant of the true guide"— and, exhorting him to strive in the conversion of his people, conferred on him the title of "Pahtán," —a term which the Afghan book-makers explain to be a Syrian word signifying the rudder of a ship, as the new proselyte was henceforth to be the guide of his people in the way they should go.'

Page 17. 'At what period the Afghans of Ghor moved forward and settled in the Kandahar country, which is now their home, is not known. It appears, however, from the writings of the early Muhammadan historians, that in the first century of their era....'

Page 19. 'Kais, they say, married a daughter of that Khalid-bin-Walíd who brought his people the first tidings of the Prophet and his doctrine, and by her he had three sons, whom he named respectively, Saraban, Batan, and Ghurghusht....

The Afghans Proper—the Bani Israíl, as they call themselves in special distinction to all other divisions of the nation—class themselves as the descendants of Saraban through his two sons, Sharjyún and Khrishyún.'

Page 24. 'By Muhammadans of Asia Minor and the Western countries the Afghan is usually called Sulemáni.'

13

The **Cyclopædia of India** and of Eastern and Southern Asia, by Surgeon General Edward Balfour, vol. I, Third Edition (Bernard Quaritch, London 1885)

page 31 *(Under the heading 'Afghanistan')*: 'Pukhtun is the national appellation of the Afghans proper; but Afghans and Pathans also designate themselves Ban-i-Israel, and some claim direct descent from Saul, king of Israel. Pukhtun is the individual, and Pukhtana the collective name of the Afghans. This word is described as of Hebrew (Ibrani) origin, though some of them say it has a Syrian (Suriani) source, and signifies delivered, set free. The term Afghan is also said to have the same signification. One tradition is that the mother of Afghan or Afghana, on his being born exclaimed, 'Afghana', 'I am free,' and gave him this name; another tradition is that in the pangs of labour she exclaimed: 'Afghan, Afghan,' or 'Fighan, Fighan,' words which in the Persian mean woe! grief! alas! Afghan is claimed as the designation only of the descendants of Kais.

The term Pathan is said to be from Pihtan, a titular appellation alleged to have been bestowed by Mahomed on an Afghan called Kais.

Their origin is involved in obscurity. But several writers consider them to be descendants of one of the ten tribes of Israel; and this is an opinion of some Afghans themselves. A few authors consider that this nation is not of Jewish origin, but that those who introduced the Mahomedan religion amongst them were converted Jews.'

Page 34. 'Among the Yusufzai, no man sees his wife till the marriage ceremonies are completed; and with all the Bardurani there is great reserve between the time when the parties are betrothed and the marriage. Some of them live with their future father-in-law, and earn their bread by their services, as Jacob did Rachel, without ever seeing the object of their wishes.....

Among the Afghans, as among the Jews, it is thought incumbent on the brother of the deceased to marry his widow, and it is a mortal affront to the brother for any other person to marry her without his consent.'

14

Narrative of a **Mission to Bokhara**, in the years 1843-1845, to ascertain the Fate of Colonel Stoddart and Captain Conolly, by the Rev. Joseph Wolff, D.D. LL.D., Vol. 1, second edition, revised (John W. Parker, London {1845} M.DCCC.XLV.)

Page 7. 'From various conversations with Affghauns in Khorassaun and elsewhere, I learnt that some of them are proud of an origin from the children of Israel, but I doubt the truth of that partial tradition.'

Page 13. 'All the Jews of Tūrkistaun assert that the Tūrkomauns are the descendants of Togarmah, one of the sons of Gomer, mentioned in Genesis x. 3.'

Pages 14-16. 'The Jews in Bokhara are 10,000 in number. The chief rabbi assured me that Bokhara is the Habor, and Balkh the Halah, of the 2nd Kings, xvii.6; but that in the reign of Genghis Khan they lost all their written accounts. At Balkh the Mussulman mullahs assured me that it was built by a son of Adam, that its first name had been Hanakh, and afterwards Halah, though later writers called it Balakh, or Balkh. The Jews, both of Balkh and Samarcand, assert that Tūrkistaun is the land of Nod, and Balkh where Nod "once stood."...... The tradition is an old one at Bokhara, that some of the Ten Tribes are in China. I tried the Jews here on various points of Scriptural interpretation, particularly that important one in Isaiah vii.14 -- עלמה Virgin. They translated it as we Christians do, and they are in total ignorance of the important controversy between Jews and Christians on that point.

I obtained a passport from the King after this most interesting sojourn, and then crossed the Oxus, and arrived after a few days at Balkh; and from that city, where I also communed with the dispersed of Israel, I proceeded to Muzaur....... Some Affghauns claim a descent from Israel. According to them, Affghaun was the nephew of Asaph, the son of Berachia, who built the Temple of Solomon. The descendants of this Affghaun, being Jews, were carried into Babylon by Nebuchadnezzar, from whence they were removed to the mountain of Ghoree, in Affghanistaun, but in the time of Muhammed turned Muhammedans. They exhibit a book, *Majmooa Alansab*, or Collection of Genealogies, written in Persian.'

Page 17. 'Hence I passed to Peshawr. Here I had also the singular book read to me of the origin of the Affghauns, the Poshtoo Book of Khan Jehaun Loote. The account in this book agrees with that given in the MSS., *Teemur Nameh* and *Ketaub Ansabee Muhakkek Toose*. I thought the general physiognomy not Jewish, but I was wonderfully struck with the resemblance that the Youssuf Szeye and the Khaibaree, two of their tribes, bear to the Jews. The Kaffre Seeah Poosh, if Affghauns, vary widely from the rest of their nation. Many travellers have thought them the descendants from Alexander's army, but they do not say so.'

Page 18. 'I always thought that the Kaffre Seeah Poosh were descendants of Israel; and some of the learned Jews of Samarcand are of my opinion.'

Pages 19-20. 'Captain Riley, I was surprised to find, looked on the Affghauns as of Jewish descent.'

Page 58. 'I spent six days with the children of Rechab (Beni Arhab)...... With them were children of Israel of the tribe of Dan, who reside near Terim in Hatramawt, who expect, in common with the children of Rechab, the speedy arrival of the Messiah in the clouds of heaven.'

Page 131. 'It is very remarkable that the Prophet Ezekiel, in the twenty-seventh chapter, fourteenth verse, gives an exact description of the trade carried on by the Tūrkomauns with the inhabitants of Bokhara, Khiva, and Khokand. The Prophet says: "They of the house of Togarmah (i.e. the Tūrkomauns) traded in thy fairs with horses and horsemen, and mules." The Tūrkomauns to this day, like the Swiss Guards, are mercenaries, and let themselves out for a few tengas a day. It is also remarkable, that I frequently heard the Tūrkomauns call themselves Toghramah, and the Jews call them Togarmah.

Viewing the hosts of camels coming with merchandise from Cashmeer, Cabūl, Khokand, Khetay, and Orenbourg, the passage of Isaiah 1x.6, comes forcibly on the mind, where the Prophet says: "The multitude of camels shall cover thee, the dromedaries of Midian and Ephah; all they from Sheba shall come: they shall bring gold and incense." Mentioning gold, I must not forget, that near Samarcand there are gold mines and turquoises.'

Pages 236-237. 'A few words on the Chaldeans in the mountains of Kurdistaun. These Chaldeans, as the late lamented Dr. Grant well observed, are of Jewish origin, though I cannot go so far as to affirm that they are of the Ten Tribes, since they do not know their own genealogy. They are now mostly Christians...... They resemble mostly the Protestants of Germany and England, for they have neither images nor monasteries, and their priests are married. The episcopal dignity, however, is hereditary, as well as that of the Patriarch, and at the time the mother of the patriarch becomes pregnant, she abstains from drinking wine and eating meat; and in case that a son is born, he is the patriarch, and if a daughter, she is obliged to observe eternal virginity.'

15

The **Lost Tribes** and the Saxons of the East and of the West, with new Views of Buddhism, and Translations of Rock-Records in India, by George Moore, M.D. (Longman, Green, Longman, and Roberts, London {1861} MDCCCLXI)

Page 143. 'We are attracted at once to a country of vast importance in the present aspect of the East, and the more interesting to us, as we there find a people who profess to be the Beni-Israel, or descendants of the Ten Tribes, namely, Afghanistan and the adjacent countries.'

Pages 145-146. 'The prominent reasons for thinking that certain classes of the people of Bokhara and Afghanistan are of Israelitish origin are these:— 1st. Their personal resemblance to the Hebrew family. Thus Dr. Wolff, the Jewish missionary, says: "I was wonderfully struck with the resemblance of the Youssoufszye [tribe of Joseph], and the Khybere, two of their tribes, to the Jews." Moorcroft also says of the Khyberes, "They are tall, and of singularly Jewish cast of features." 2nd. They have been named by themselves Beni-Israel, children of Israel, from time immemorial. 3rd. The names of their tribes are Israelitish, especially that of Joseph, which includes Ephraim and Manasseh. In the Book of Revelation the tribe of Joseph stands for Ephraim. (Rev. vii. 6,8.) In Numbers xxxvi.5, Moses speaks of Manasseh as "the tribe of the sons of Joseph;" so that it is clear that both Manasseh and Ephraim were known by the name of the tribe of Joseph. 4th. The Hebrew names of places and persons in Afghanistan are of far greater frequency than can be accounted for through Mahometan association; and, indeed, these names existed before the Afghans became Mahometans. 5th. All accounts agree that they inhabited the mountains of Ghore from a very remote antiquity. It is certain that the princes of Ghore belonged to the Afghan tribe of Sooree, and that their dynasty was allowed to be of very great antiquity even in the eleventh century. "They seem early to have possessed the mountains of Solimaun or Solomon, comprehending all the southern mountains of Afghanistan." (Elphinstone.) 6th. Afghan is the name given to their nation by others, the name they give their nation is Pushtoon, and Drs. Carey and Marshman assert that the Pushtoon language has more Hebrew roots than any other.'

Pages 147-148. 'The antiquity of the name of the country Cabul, or Cabool, is then established; and it is also shown that some peculiar people known as "The Tribes," and "The Noble Tribes," dwelt there at a very remote period. There is, therefore, good evidence that the present inhabitants of Cabul may be justified in asserting that from the earliest period of history they and their ancestors have occupied Cabul, and that from time immemorial they have been known as "The Tribes." That is to say, Israelitish tribes, such as they now assume themselves to be. .... According to Sir W. Jones, the best Persian authorities agree with them in their account of their origin; and resident and competent authorities, such as Sir John Malcolm, and the missionary Mr. Chamberlain, after full investigation, assure us that many of the Afghans are undoubtedly of the seed of Abraham.'

16

The Works of **Flavius Josephus**; comprising the Antiquities of the Jews; a **History of the Jewish Wars**, and Life of Flavius Josephus; Written by Himself. Translated by William Whiston, A.M., Professor of mathematics in the University of Cambridge (Willoughby & Co. London 1840)

Page 223 '...the ten tribes are beyond Euphrates till now, and are an immense multitude, and not to be estimated by numbers.'

17

A personal narrative of a visit to **Ghuzni, Kabul, and Afghanistan**, and of a Residence at the Court of Dost Mohamed: with Notices of Runjit Sing, Khiva, and the Russian Expedition, by G. T. Vigne Esq. F.G.S. (Whittaker & Co. London 1840)

Pages 166-167. 'Moollah Khoda Dad, a person learned in the history of his countrymen, read to me, from the Mujma-ul-Unsab (collection of genealogies), the following short account of their origin. They say, that the eldest of Jacob's sons was Judah, whose eldest son was Osruk, who was the father of Oknur, the father of Moalib, the father of Farlai, the father of Kys, the father of Talut, the father of Ermiah, the father of Afghana, whence the name of Afghans. He was contemporary with Nebuchadnezzar, called himself Bin-i-Israel, and had forty sons, whose names there is no occasion to insert. His thirty-fourth descendant, in a direct line, after a period of two thousand years, was Kys. From Kys, who lived in the time of the prophet Mahomed, there have been sixty-six generations. Sulum, the eldest son of Afghana, who lived at Sham [Damascus], left that place, and came to Ghura Mishkon, a country near Herat; and his descendants gradually extended themselves over the country now called Afghanistan.'

18

A **Cyclopædia of Geography** Descriptive and Physical, forming a New General Gazetteer of the World and Dictionary of Pronunciation, by James Bryce, M.A., F.G.S. (Richard Griffin and Co. London and Glasgow 1856)

page 11. 'The name Afghan is not used by the people themselves; they call themselves Pooshtoon, and in the plural Pooshtaûneh, from which, perhaps, comes the name Putan, or Patan, given to them in India. They trace their origin to Saul, King of Israel, calling themselves, Ben-i-Israel. According to Sir A. Burnes, their tradition is, that they were transplanted by the King of Babylon from the Holy Land to Ghoré, lying to the N.W. of Cabool, and lived as Jews till A.D. 682, when they were converted to Mahometanism by an Arab chief, Khaled-ibn-Abdalla, who had married a daughter of an Afghan chief. No historical evidence has ever been adduced in support of this origin, and it is perhaps a mere invention, founded upon the facts mentioned in 2 Kings xviii.11. However this may be, all travellers agree that the people differ strikingly from the neighbouring nations; and have, among themselves, one common origin. They are said, by some, to resemble Jews very much in form and feature; and they are divided into several tribes, inhabiting separate territories, and remaining almost unmixed.'

19

History of Afghanistan, from the Earliest Period to the Outbreak of the War of 1878, by Colonel G. B. Malleson, C.S.I. (W.H. Allen & Co. London, 1878)

Page 39. 'I turn now to the people of Afghánistán, to the tribes who occupy the country, and who command the passes. The subject has been treated at great length by Mountstuart Elphinstone, by Ferrier—who quotes largely from Abdúllah Khán, of Herát,—by Bellew, and by many others.

Following Abdúllah Khán and other Afghán writers, Ferrier is disposed to believe that the Afgháns represent the lost ten tribes, and to claim for them descent from Saul, King of Israel. Amongst other writers concurring in this view may be mentioned the honoured name of Sir William Jones. On the other hand, Professor Dorn, of Kharkov, who examined the subject at length, rejects this theory. Mountstuart Elphinstone classes it in the same category as the theory of the descent of the Romans from the Trojans. The objections to Abdúllah Khán's view have been recently expressed, fittingly and forcibly, by Professor Dowson, in a letter to the *Times*. "If," writes that gentleman, "it were worthy of consideration, it is still inconsistent with the notion that the Afgháns are descendants of the lost ten tribes. Saul was of the tribe of Benjamin, and that tribe was not one of the lost ten. There remains the question of feature. This, no doubt, has its weight, but cannot prevail against the more important question of language." Professor Dowson then proceeds to show that the Afghán language has no trace of Hebrew in it, and concludes by pronouncing the supposition that in the course of time the whole Afghán race could have changed their language as "too incredible."

20

History of the Afghans by J. P. Ferrier, translated from the original unpublished manuscript by Captain William Jesse (John Murray, London, 1858)

Page 1. '... the majority of Eastern writers consider them to be the descendants of one of the ten tribes of Israel— and this is the opinion of the Afghans themselves.'

Page 4. '... the Afghans, however, think that they have evidence of their Jewish origin in the following tradition. When Nadir Shah, marching to the conquest of India, arrived at Peshawur, the chiefs of the tribe of Yoosoofzyes presented him with a Bible written in Hebrew, and several articles that had been used in their ancient worship which they had preserved; these articles were at once recognised by the Jews who followed the camp.'

Page 6. 'Being incompetent to decide which is right, we shall adopt the opinion of Abdullah Khan of Herat as the one most deserving of credit, and we will precede it by giving his view of the manner in which the Afghans were brought to Afghanistan. The following is a translation of his manuscript:

"..... Malek Thalut (Saul) king of the Jews had two sons, Afghan and Djalut— the first was the father of the Afghan nation and gave his name to it. After the reigns of David and Solomon, who succeeded Saul, anarchy divided the Jewish tribes, and this continued to the period at which Bouktun Nasr took Jerusalem, massacred 70,000 Jews, and after destroying that city led the surviving inhabitants captives to Babylon. Subsequently to this disaster the Afghan tribe, struck with terror, fled from Judea and settled in Arabia: here they remained some considerable time, but as pasturage and water were scarce, and both man and beast suffered extreme privation, some of the tribe determined to emigrate to Hindostan. The branch of the Abdalees continued to reside in Arabia, and during the caliphat of Aboo Bekr their chiefs allied themselves to a powerful sheikh, by name Khaled ibn Velid, of the tribe of Korech. ..... at the period when the Arabs subjugated Persia the Abdalees left Arabia and settled in this new conquest, establishing themselves in the provinces of Fars and Kerman, and here they remained until Genghis Khan invaded those districts. The tyrannical proceedings of this conqueror weighed with such terrible effect on the population, that the Abdalees quitted Persia and, passing by the Mekrane, Scinde, and Mooltan, arrived in India; but the results of this new migration were not more fortunate, for they were scarcely settled here when their neighbours made war upon, and forced them to leave the plains and inhabit the rugged mountains of Suleiman, considered as the cradle of the tribe, and called by them Kooh-Khasseh. The whole Afghan nation was brought together by the arrival of the Abdalees in the Suleiman mountains, and then consisted of twenty-four tribes, of which, as it has been already observed, Afghan, the son of Saul, was the father: this prince had three sons, named Tsera-Bend, Argoutch, and Kerlen, and each of them was the father of eight sons, who gave their names to the twenty-four tribes.

"The following is the manner in which they are classed: —

Sons of Tsera-Bend	Names of the Tribes
Abdal	Abdalees
Yoosoof	Yoosoofzyes
Baboor	Baboorees
Wezir	Wezirees
Lohooan	Lohooanees
Beritch	Beritchees
Khooguian	Khooguianees
Chiran	Chiranees
Sons of Argoutch	**Names of the Tribes**
Ghildj	Ghildjzyes
Kauker	Kaukerees
Djumourian	Djumourianees
Storian	Storianees
Pen	Penees
Kass	Kassees
Takan	Takanees
Nassar	Nassarees
Sons of Kerlen	**Names of the Tribes**
Khattak	Khattakees
Soor	Soorees
Afreed	Afreedees
Toor	Toorees
Zaz	Zazees
Bab	Babees
Benguech	Benguechees
Lendeh-poor	Lendeh-poorees'

21

History of the Afghans translated from the Persian of Neamet Ullah, by Bernhard Dorn, Ph.D. FOR. M.R.A.S. M.T.C., Part 1 & 2 (J. Murray, London, 1829)

Part 1- page 23. 'Davud treated the two afflicted widows with the utmost kindness; and Heaven blessed them each with an accomplished son, born at the same hour; of whom the one was called Berkhia; the other, Ermia......

Each of them was blessed with an accomplished son. Berkhia

called his Asif: Ermia's son was called Afghana.'

Page 24. 'God blessed Asif with eighteen, and Afghana with forty sons; whose posterity, but more particularly that of the latter, continued increasing in such a degree, that no tribe of the Israelites equalled them.'

Page 25. '..... God permitted Bokhtnasser to subjugate the territories of Sham, to rase Jerusalem, and vanquish the Israelites, so as to carry their families into captivity and slavery, and drive all those who had faith in the Tora into exile;...... He reduced the whole of Sham to his subjection; carrying away the Israelites, whom he settled in the mountainous districts of Ghor, Ghazneen, Kabul, Candahar, Koh Firozeh,....'

Page 37. 'Mestoufi, the author of the Tareekh Kozeida, and the author of the Mujmul Ansab, furnish the following records. When the lustre of Mohammed's charming countenance had arisen, and Khaled had been ennobled by embracing the Mohammedan faith, a large number of Arabs and various people repaired to Medina, and were induced, by the splendor of the Mohammedan light, to embrace Islamism. At this time, Khaled sent a letter to the Afghans who had been settled in the mountainous countries about Ghor ever since the time of the expulsion of the Israelites by Bokhtnasser, and informed them of the appearance of the last of the Prophets. On this letter reaching them, several of their chiefs departed for Medina; the mightiest of whom, and of the Afghan people, was Kais, whose pedigree ascends in a series of thirty-seven degrees to Talut of forty-five to Ibrahim, and of six hundred and three to Adam. The author of the Mujmul Ansab traces it as follows:- Pedigree of Abd Ulrasheed Kais, who is known by the surname Pathan: Kais ben Isa, ben Salool, ben Otba, ben Naeem, ben Morra, ben Gelundur, ben Iskunder, ben Reman, ben Ain, ben Mehlool, ben Salem, ben Selah, ben Farood, ben Ghan, ben Fahlool, ben Karam, ben Amal, ben Hadifa, ben Minhal, ben Kais, ben Ailem, ben Ismuel, ben Harun, ben Kumrood, ben Abi, ben Zaleeb, ben Tullal, ben Levi, ben Amel, ben Tarej, ben Arzund, ben Mundool, ben Saleem, ben Afghana, ben Irmia, ben Sarool, called Melik (King) Talut, ben Kais, ben Otba, ...'

Page 38. 'The Prophet lavished all sorts of blessings upon them; and having ascertained the name of each individual, and remarked that Kais was an Hebrew name, whereas they themselves were Arabs, he gave Kais the name Abd Ulrasheed........ their attachment to the Faith would, in strength, be like the wood upon which they lay the keel when constructing a ship, which wood the seamen call Pathan: on this account he conferred upon Abd Ulrasheed the title of Pathan also.....

The Prophet at length dismissed Abd Ulrasheed to return to Ghor and the adjacent Kohistan, there to propagate the new faith, and to direct the infidels to it.'

Part 2- page 63 (Under word 'Suleimani'). 'Muhabbat Khan tells us, that they are called so by the Arabs in consequence of their belonging to the adherents and followers of King Solomon.'

Pages 63-64. 'Bani Afghanah, Bani Afghan; that is, Children of Asif, Israel, Afghanah, or Afghan. These names are mentioned by Fareed Uddeen Ahmad, in his Risalah Ansab Afaghinah, where we find the following passage:—"When, in the course of time, Bokhtnassr the magician, who subdued the Bani Israel and the territories of Syria, and sacked Jerusalem, led the Children of Israel into captivity and slavery, and carried off with him several tribes of this people who were attached to the Law of Moses, and ordered them to adore him for God, and to abandon the creed of their fathers, they did not consent to this: upon which, he put two thousand of the wisest and most skilful of them to death, and ordered the rest to quit Syria and his dominions. Part of them, who had a chief, were led by him out of Bokhtnassr's dominions, and conducted to the Kohistan of Ghor, where their descendants settled. Their number increased daily; and people called them Bani Israel, Bani Asif, and Bani Afghanah."

Page 64. 'Fareed Uddeen Ahmed, in the beginning of his discourse, says on this point: "Concerning the denomination,

'Afghan,' some have written, that they, after their expulsion, ever bearing in mind their wonted abode, uttered bewailings and lamentations (افغان Afghan), and were on that account called 'Afghan.'" See Sir J. Malcolm's *History of Persia*, Vol. I. p. 101, where the same derivation of this word is mentioned....

Farid Uddeen Ahmed mentions, that in standard works, as in the *Tareekh Afghani, Tareekh Ghori,* and others, it is asserted that the Afghans were, for the greater part, Israelites, and some Copts. See also *Abul Fazl*, P. ii. p. 178: "Some Afghans consider themselves to be of Egyptian extraction; asserting, that when the Children of Israel returned from Jerusalem to Egypt, this tribe emigrated to Hindoostan."

Page 65. 'The Afghans, according to almost all the Oriental historians, believe themselves to be descended from the Jews; an opinion that was even adopted, or considered probable, by some modern writers...... The use of Jewish names, which the Afghans employ, is undoubtedly attributable to their being Mussulmans..... The only proof that might be adduced in favour of their pretended Jewish extraction, is the striking likeness of the Afghan features to the Jewish; which has been admitted, even by such as do not pay the least attention to their claim to a Jewish origin. Sir John Malcolm's words on this subject are: "Although their right to this proud descent (from the Jews) is very doubtful, it is evident, from their personal appearance, and many of their usages, that they are a distinct race from the Persians, Tartars, and Indians; and this alone seems to give some credibility to a statement which is contradicted by many strong facts, and of which no direct proof has been produced. If an inference could be drawn from the features of a nation resembling those of another, the Cashmirians would certainly, by their Jewish features, prove a Jewish origin, which not only Bernier, but Forster, and perhaps others, have remarked."

Pages 65-66. 'Now, although Forster does not approve of the opinion of Bernier, tracing the descent of the Cashmirians to the

exiled Jewish tribes, yet he confesses, that, when among the
Cashmirians, he thought himself to be amongst a nation of Jews.'

22

Dictionary of Geography, Descriptive, Physical,
Statistical, And Historical, Forming a Complete General
Gazetteer of the World, By Alex. Keith Johnston,
F.R.S.E., F.R.G.S., F.G.S., Second Edition, thoroughly
revised and corrected (Longman, Brown, Green, and
Longmans, London {1855} MDCCLV)

Page 250 *(Under word 'Cashmere')*: 'The natives are of a tall robust
frame of body, with manly features—the women full-formed and
handsome, with aquiline nose and features, resembling the Jewish.'

Index: